MEDITATION
IN A
CHANGING WORLD

An introduction to individual and group meditation

William Bloom

Other books by William Bloom:

Devas, Fairies and Angels

First Steps — An Introduction to Spiritual Practice

The Sacred Magician

Sacred Times

The New Age (editor)

The Seeker's Guide (edited with John Button)

*Personal Identity, National Identity
   and International Relations*

Money, Heart and Mind

The Christ Speaks

Psychic Protection

MEDITATION
IN A
CHANGING WORLD

William Bloom

Illustrated by Marko Pogacnik

GOTHIC IMAGE
PUBLICATIONS

This edition first published 1996 by
Gothic Image Publications
7 High Street
Glastonbury, Somerset
BA6 9DP

Cover illustration by Marko Pogacnik

Text design and production by
Mentor DTP
Bruton, Somerset
with revisions for this edition by
Abbey Press
Glastonbury

Printed and bound in Great Britain by
WBC Book Manufacturers
Bridgend, Mid-Glamorgan

A catalogue record for this book is available
from the British Library
ISBN 0 906362 37 7

Dedication
For James, Hannah, Ossian, Michael, Josie and William.

Acknowledgements

I have to thank several groups and friends for their help and support:

The Glastonbury meditation group, the Findhorn Foundation and the Meitheal Community in Ireland, where the major portion of this book was written.

For invaluable editorial advice and enlightening comments, Roy Arbuckle, Ken Carey, Eileen Caddy, Gordon Davidson, Caro Hall, Frances Howard-Gordon, Corinne McLaughlin, Cary Meehan and Frances Moore.

For the illustrations, Marko Pogacnik. For those who do not know his work, Marko Pogacnik is Slovenia's leading landscape sculptor; some people will buy this book for his illustrations and not for my prose.

I must make a special mention of the support, loyalty and enthusiasm of Frances Howard-Gordon and Jamie George, who, amongst other things, are my publishers — given difficult circumstances, their love and generosity of spirit has been extraordinary and I am very grateful.

And a final thank-you to Cary for her love and faith which supported me.

For the second edition
Over the five years since first writing this book I have come to understand better the everyday needs of people approaching a meditation practice for the first time, particularly the problems and challenges that obstruct during the first weeks. For illumination, enlightenment and inspiration, I am grateful to all the groups and students who have worked with me.

inspiration, I am grateful to all the groups and students who have worked with me.

One night, before leading a large retreat, I dreamt that I was in the jungle playing with a friendly clan of gorillas. Suddenly this enormous gorilla — the mother-father of all gorillas — arrived and led me away. We sat down together, directly facing each other and I felt this wonderful, safe and enfolding quality emanating from her stomach. It was very powerful. At the same time she looked into my eyes with great love, compassion and joy. She held me like that for ten minutes. 'This is the way,' she communicated, 'to hold a retreat.' The glow of that lesson remains with me. I am grateful to that gorilla.

I also need to say thank you to Sabrina for her consistent help and encouragement.

Contents

		Page
Introduction		1
1.	The Nature of Meditation	5
INDIVIDUAL MEDITATION		17
2.	First Principles	19
3.	Location and Beginning	25
4.	Centering	31
5.	Alignment	41
6.	Review	57
7.	Expansion of Consciousness	69
8.	Awareness	81
9.	Service, Invocation and Radiation	85
10.	More General Comments and Advice	93
GROUP MEDITATION		101
11.	Why Group Meditation?	103
12.	Individual Meditation in Groups	109
13.	Group Meditation for a Common Purpose	111
14.	Leading Group Meditations	119
APPENDIX		133
Practical Hints on Relaxation and Stress Control		135
Mantrams, Prayers and Affirmations		138
Meditation of the Dove		152
Revision Notes		155
The Lunar Cycle and Solar Festivals		160
Booklist		175
Afterword		177

Introduction

This book has been written for anyone who wants to start a meditation practice or for anyone, already meditating, who wants some clarity and hints at what their next steps might be. My purpose is not to persuade anyone that meditation is a good and wonderful thing — although, of course, I think it is. My purpose is to make as clear and as simple as possible what happens in meditation, how it happens and why it happens. I want this book to be a clear, helpful and practical guide. I do not assume that you the reader are a mystic, believe in God, or have any other particular belief system. I only assume a genuine curiosity and an open investigative mind.

Over two decades I have led, participated in and learned from many different meditation groups. In all of these groups similar questions have arisen about the nature and purpose of meditation, and there have been many different and illuminating discussions. What has been clear in all these discussions, is that we now have a single language which allows us all to talk together about meditation whatever our backgrounds. Today we can directly discuss the nature of energy and of consciousness in relation to meditation and I use this language in the book.

There are many different schools of meditation, and there are great similarities and convergences in all their teachings. Where they differ is in the particular aspect of meditation upon which they focus. Some schools, for example, are mainly concerned with the techniques of achieving calm and silence. Other schools are focused upon exercises and attitudes of self-awareness. And yet others, for instance, are concerned purely with consciousness expansion. I myself have been particularly inspired by the approaches of the eastern schools of Vepassana, Raja and Agni Yoga, and the western approach of the Kabbalists and the Christian mystics of the Ignatian school.

Of course when practitioners of the many different schools of meditation meditate together, there is no conflict. This is not simply because they are silent, but because they are sharing an experience which is universally the same whenever people deliberately take inner quiet. Just as we all share similar physical features — torso, limbs, head — we also all share a similar psyche, a similar inner psychology. When we meditate we, therefore, share a common experience. It is the universality of this experience which also makes a book like this possible.

It is one of the features of the emerging spiritual culture that, freed from the constraints of having to adhere to one particular religion or belief system, there is a growing movement of people who meditate. More and more of us are choosing to meditate because in the privacy of our own lives it suits us. This large movement towards meditation is due to its inherent freedom — there is no one in the silence telling us what to do — and also to the mayhem of contemporary life which evokes from us a new need to find silence and harmony with ourselves and with the planet.

Some schools of meditation presume a certain belief about the nature of the cosmos and the nature of deity, but meditation, in fact, is precisely a totally private and individual way of discovering for ourself the nature and dimensions of existence. In meditation we have the opportunity to explore freely the nature and the dimensions of everything. Day by day, meditation provides a voyage of inner discovery. This discovery may sometimes be one purely of personal peace, while at other times it is surely the most profound and illuminating learning experience that is available.

Meditation in my experience can be practised by anyone and can be learnt by anyone. It is a natural aspect of everyone's life to daydream or to be contemplative. Meditation is simply a matter of staying in that relaxed and contemplative atmosphere, but instead of day-dreaming we are awake, focused and self-aware.

As I neared completion of the first edition of this book, a friend asked me what I was doing. I told her. She smiled and exclaimed:

'A whole book! Can't you just tell people to be quiet and listen?'

Her point is indeed fair. Many people come to meditation precisely in this way, simply by taking periods of silence and listening. In fact, that is how I first started to meditate. In my early twenties, before I went to work in the morning, I used to stop for fifteen minutes in a local church that was always empty and where no one bothered me, to calm and gather myself. And thus, over a while, instinctively I found that I was a meditator. A clear map, however, in simple language of what happens in meditation and what else I could do in it would have helped me. In a sense, then, this book is written for the me of twenty years ago. I hope with all my heart that this book helps you, the reader. I have the deepest respect for each individual's unique process and path. My object is not to preach or to constrain, but simply to share a helpful map.

Enjoy the extraordinary wonderful journey. May all the blessings of enlightenment and illumination be on our path.

1. The Nature of Meditation

In this first chapter I want to provide an immediate overview of the whole subject. We will then explore it in greater detail.

The Purpose of Meditation

The reality for all of us is that we are complex and multifaceted creatures. We each of us have many different psychological aspects, moods and attitudes, which appear in different situations and different relationships. It is possible to simplify these many different parts of ourselves and to say that at the very least we are dualistic beings. We have an outer personality — developed in our families, schools and societies, and fuelled by our need to survive and to feel safe — and we also have an inner personality. It is fairly easy to identify the outer personality. We use it all the time. It takes us through our leisure, our relationships and our work. It has strong feelings, attitudes and beliefs. It has very distinct patterns.

We also have an inner personality. It is subtle, less noisy and less obvious, but it is there and known by each of us. It is a secret place of silence and in this inner personality we are truly ourselves. When we experience this inner part we are truly ourself, more wise, more loving and understanding, more harmonic with the purpose of all life. From this part of ourself we each have that very private and secret sense that we have a unique gift and blessing for this world. Increasingly, in contemporary psychology the existence of this core self is being recognised as the organising dynamic of the personality.

In my book *First Steps* I wrote this about it:

> 'There are not only different names for it: soul, spirit,
> psyche, inner self, higher self, core self, multi-
> dimensional self. There are also different ideas about
> it.
>
> Where there is agreement between the different
> belief systems is in the idea that the *core self* is the
> major organising principle of who we are. Behind the
> psychological scenes the core self takes us forward
> through our lives with a consistent and coherent
> dynamic. How this dynamic manifests varies from
> person to person. It is usual to accept that the core self
> organises our lives so as to help us fulfil our true
> potential. And it is further assumed that to fulfil our
> true potential means becoming wiser, more integrated
> and more loving.
>
> Why the core self does this and what the core self
> does after death and before birth is a subject of much
> discussion. The options include:
> • The core self is a complex part of the biological
> mechanism of the human being and, at death,
> disintegrates in the same way as the physical body.
> • The core self reincarnates, life by life building up
> a wiser, more integrated and loving identity, until
> finally it either dissolves in bliss or becomes a
> transcendent and eternal liberated consciousness.
> • The core self is a peak in the vast ocean of the
> collective unconscious of humanity, finally dissolving
> back into that unconscious, but also serving to evolve
> and transform the totality.
>
> Only you the individual, in the privacy of your own
> senses and intuitions, can decide about its true nature.'

In meditation, we allow this inner personality to come fully present. The inner self can only come present if our outer personality is silent. Meditation takes the outer personality into an atmosphere of silence. Meditation allows the core self to come present. And meditation helps us to be perfectly aware and focused as all this happens.

Let's discuss this duality for a while in the framework of consciousness. It is clear that we have a certain consciousness for our daily lives. There is a certain way that we perceive, experience and respond to our lives. This consciousness, everyday consciousness, is coloured by the kind of characters we are and the kinds of situation in which we place ourselves. This consciousness, however, changes. It may change when we experience music, or dance, or landscape, or loving relationship. We perceive, experience and respond in new and different ways.

In meditation, with our body and feelings and thoughts in harmonic silence, we allow ourselves to experience a different form of consciousness. We allow this different form of consciousness into our experience. Or, put another way, we *expand* our consciousness so that it has new awareness. We do not lose awareness of everything we are and have been, but we expand our awareness into new perceptions and experience.

All of this is to say that, in meditation, we become who we truly are. To be more exact, it might be better to say:

In meditation we develop awareness of who we really are and then slowly we become it.

Resistance and Avoidance

Every meditator—with angels as exceptions—experiences resistance to being quiet and in silence. This resistance manifests, for example, in physical pain, uncontrolled or obsessive thoughts, overwhelming feelings of anxiety and a sense of worthlessness or time-wasting. These experiences happen especially to beginners, but they also happen to people who have been sitting in seclusion for decades. The major difference between the beginner and the experienced practitioner is that the beginner may be dismayed and even stop the meditation practice, whereas the experienced practitioner simply accepts the experience and continues to hold focus in the centre of it all.

This resistance is normal and also perfectly logical. Due to our prolonged infancies and the wounds we endure whilst adjusting to the realities of human life, we are all damaged creatures. Most of the time we move forward with no awareness of our damage except in crisis or when we collapse into illness. In meditation, as we begin to silence ourselves, the wounds and anxieties that are normally ignored surface in our consciousness. The tension we normally endure is suddenly felt in our backs, thighs and shoulders. Our lack of self-worth manifests as complete distrust in what we are doing as we sit attempting to be quiet. Our minds throttle forward in a frenzy of obsessive thoughts which our subconscious throws up to distract us.

We need to be realistic about the strength of this resistance when we begin a meditation practice and realistic about the fact that it will recur all through our lives. For most people starting a meditation practice is like stopping smoking or going on a diet. It is easy for the first two or three days, but then we lose the discipline finding cunning excuses to rationalise our avoidance. The only way to ride this resistance is to use motivation and self-discipline. This is one of those paradoxes of meditation: we look for silence and surrender, but to achieve it we need motivation and discipline. That is just the way it is.

If we are starting a practice, therefore, we need to be very clear that this is what we want to do. The motivational energy of a *whim* to meditate will not carry us through. We have to appreciate that to find those regular minutes every day require a sacrifice of other minutes. Regular meditation intrudes into our everyday life. It is a huge signpost saying that we are moving our consciousness into a new direction. The rest of our life, unless already filled with a contemplative rhythm, will be irritated by the intruder and its promise of change.

Most people need about three months to slip into the rhythm of their practice; others may need only a few weeks; and yet others a couple of years. The point is simply to accept the reality that it will take some time. There are very few things in life worth doing that can be done successfully at first try. It takes time to learn the basic skills and time to develop them. The basic technique of meditation is to hold a focused awareness in the midst of anything.

The beginner, encountering all the inner noise and distraction, often says, 'This isn't meditation. This is a waste of time. I cannot do it. I am stopping this.' This particular inner voice, the cunning and patronising judge, needs also to be ignored. The patronising judge is part of the avoidance pattern that does not want us to be silent and to become conscious of who we really are. The avoidance pattern does not want us to become aware of the wounds and of the layers of pretence that allow us to survive in human society.

If we hold to a daily rhythm sooner or later we will experience the 'noise' of our bodies, feelings and thoughts losing its jagged irritation. Our everyday personality, instead of resisting the silence with jagged edges and grating peaks of interference, finally slips into a harmonic of calm waves in a wide, wide ocean. At last we are breathing calm and everything within us is also breathing and in a settled rhythm. It is a natural silence. It is not dead or inert, but the gentle soothing pulsation of inner life. Everything feels relaxed. And in the centre of the relaxation is the meditator's awareness, focused and aware, monarch in the temple of our body and psyche.

But be aware and be realistic about the resistance. I will give some hints on how to deal with this later.

The Basic Skills — Relaxation and Focus

The foundation of meditation is the ability to allow the noise of personality to calm itself into a natural harmonic whilst we simultaneously hold our focus of awareness. By holding our focus of awareness, I mean that whatever is going on in or around us, I the meditator am always able to say, 'Here I am, calm and observing.' This is the basic and the essential technique of meditation: to hold a focused awareness in the midst of anything — in the midst of mad thoughts and feelings; in the midst of noise, joy and ecstasy; in the midst of physical pain, boredom and impatience.

Whatever is happening in our meditation the core attitude is to stay present and observing. Here are two very common examples of how people lose their focus of observation.

In the first example we may be having a very uncomfortable meditation in which all kinds of inner turbulence and resistance are surfacing. We remain observing it until the inner voice of the patronising judge starts saying, 'This isn't meditation. I'm wasting my time. I should get back to the children or my work.' We listen to that voice which also carries an emotional sensation of impatience and anxiety. Instead of calmly observing the voice and the feelings, we get caught up in it. We think that we are the thinker and stop observing. We take notice of it. We identify with it. We believe it. We believe we are wasting our time. We get up and stop meditating. No! Stop! The core skill of meditation here is to remain the observer and observe the cunning judge — and stay in meditation. Compassionately observe the pattern.

A second example is when we achieve a lovely relaxed silence and begin to contemplate beautiful things. We enter into this wonderful inner world, drift off and some time later come back to consciousness. This is daydreaming. It is very pleasant and useful if we want simply to relax, but it is not meditation. If it were meditation, then we would remain observer to the daydream, rather than getting lost in it.

So we have to learn these two great skills which we practise simultaneously:
- Relax everything.
- Hold a focus as the observer.

Relaxation and attention. In this way, as everything calms we have the ability to be truly conscious, open to all that is.

But, whilst we are relaxed and focused, waves of distraction may come in sometimes overwhelming our experience and knocking us off centre. These distractions, as I have already described, are images, thoughts, feelings and physical sensations. The experienced meditator holds their focus whatever the distraction. Our greatest ally and support in this struggle is our breath.

Breath
In the very first place, observing our breath is an easy way to bring us into focus and relaxation. I always begin my own meditations simply counting my breaths to one hundred, and sometimes to two or three hundred. I know that when I have the noise of my personality in harmonic quiet, my breathing will also be calm. So I help my breathing be calm by focusing upon it, and by releasing tension in my chest, abdomen and throat. I also make certain that my breath is regular and rhythmic. In one way or another, all meditators

make sure their breathing is calm and relaxed. Some do it consciously, others unconsciously. When I feel calm, I stop giving attention to my breathing. But when irritation or distraction occurs, I consciously focus on keeping my breath calm and regular.

When irritation and distraction occur — whether painful or ecstatic — experienced meditators do three things. They stay relaxed, they stay focused and they keep breathing in a calm and regular manner. No matter how great the distraction or irritation, they keep breathing. In the contemporary jargon, we 'breath through' our process. When two consciousness workers meet and they ask each other how they are, and one replies, 'I'm breathing,' this is a meaningful communication. Reading between the lines, it says, 'I'm irritable and want to kill, but I am retaining my focus through my breath.' Or read deeper between the lines and you hear the meditator's silent mantram, *arghhh*.

Experienced meditators are extremely familiar with the inner *arghhh* as the deeper we go into meditation, the deeper are our own wounds and resistance that we contact. The most technically knowledgeable and realistic of the meditation cultures is that of northern India and Tibet where there are wonderful paintings of meditation. In these gorgeous pictures the meditator may, for example, be seen sitting serenely upon a throne of divine clouds whilst around there are angry dragons, demons and skeletons. These creatures are not external threats to the saintly contemplative. They, in fact, depict the different inner aspects of the saint's own psychology, all rising to be acknowledged and breathed through in the saint's silent work.

The Good Host and the Void

The trick, then, is not to be overwhelmed by interference. The interference — whatever its source and whether it is

physical discomfort, charming images or impatient ideas —
will seek to seduce us into giving it full attention and
believing in it. I may write knowledgeably about it, but I still
get caught sometimes. Once I recognise that I have been
caught by some interference, I take the advice that comes
from the Tibetan tradition. This Tibetan teaching advises
us, in meditation, to be a good host to everything that turns
up, to have an attitude of goodwill and compassion, not
resentment. Our mind and psyche in meditation, it tells us,
is like a large house in which we are having a party. We are
the host and it is our job to be welcoming and generous.

So I take this advice and I acknowledge the interference
as an old friend, a gate-crasher in the party of my psyche. I
congratulate it on having forced an entry and tell it that I
shall now continue with my meditation, centered and
observing.

Sometimes people talk about meditation as going into
'nothingness' or the 'void'. The meaning of this is not that
the mind and psyche become an infinite blank of nothing. It
means that the mind and psyche relax and become huge
and expansive, like the dome of the sky, like a great void. In
this dome there is room for everything, and every-thing can
be welcomed and lived with serenely and compassionately.
It is a wonderful attitude which easily embraces irritation
and interference. The house of the psyche, in which we are
the host, is immense.

The Two Major Approaches to Meditation
In many ways this is all any of us need to know about
meditation:
- Relax.
- Hold a focused awareness as the observer.
- Keep the breath moving in a calm rhythm.

Beyond those core skills, we need to be *patient* and *regular* in our practice.

If we persevere with these basic guidelines, then we shall gradually build up our meditation rhythm and momentum, and begin to enjoy the presence of true consciousness.

There is in fact one major school of meditation, Buddhist Vepassana, which says that breath and observation are all that we need to know about meditation, and to do anything else is illusory and a waste of time. Through staying calmly with the breath and observation, everything that needs to will finally arise in our awareness and we shall breathe through it, transform our attachment into detachment, and liberate our consciousness. Vepassana is very clear about this approach and if you take Vepassana instruction or do a Vepassana retreat — or that of a similar school — you will learn to sit, be silent and observe.

Different from this approach are the many traditions and teachings which are more *active* and give clear instructions on particular ways in which meditation can be used to speed up our individual paths of transformation, to give ourselves an education in cosmic consciousness and to serve the rest of our planetary community through healing and blessing. The Vepassana approach, however, would tend to say that all these active practices are part of the illusion through which we must breathe until finally our consciousness becomes still and expanded into a harmony with everything. The active meditator says that both approaches are valid.

My own experience is that there need be no conflict between the passive and the active approaches. Whichever approach we use, we always need the skill and discipline of being able to breathe through anything and remain the observer. At the same time I believe that the practitioner of Vepassana, over the decades, experiences everything that the more active meditator touches. The Vepassana practitioner allows everything to come into awareness in its own due time, whereas the active practitioner is more creative in stimulating his or her own tempo.

I would be very happy if some readers of this book read no further. Go and sit quietly for twenty minutes. Gently observe everything. When you need to, guide your breath. Do this every day and over time you will learn, on your own, all that is to be known about meditation. It will come to you as naturally as the force of gravity holds us on the earth.

How Meditation Feels

The more I meditate and listen to how other people meditate, the more I realise that the actual experience of good meditation is *felt* through the whole physical body as well as *perceived* by the psyche and mind. And I sometimes think nowadays that meditation is taught with too much of a focus on alarming words such as *attention! self-discipline! silence!* All these words are to do with mental attitudes and do not hint at the pleasant general experience which is to follow. It is true that self-discipline is needed to maintain the stance of being observer of oneself, but beyond that, when we begin to have good meditation, it is an experience that comes into the whole physical body.

This may start with different sensations and aware-nesses in the mind, but it will then radiate and move into the whole body. Good meditation feels like deep relaxation, but a quantum leap better. Look at the men and women who have a good meditation practice. They have happy bodies.

In good meditation it is possible for the mind and even the emotions to be jumping all over the place, but if you stay observant and breathing, then you will nevertheless still have a good experience. This means that you will be having two experiences at the same time: jumpy mind and emotions, *plus* relaxed body and observant, even blissful, attitude. This dual experience happens to most meditators much of the time in one way or another.

It is important to recognise all this because many beginners might think that they are getting it wrong and give up because they are experiencing a chattering mind or impatient emotions. The challenge is just to stay relaxed and watchful.

Perhaps if women had taught meditation for the last two thousand years, there would be a softer and more understanding approach to the way in which meditation is taught. More heart than head. It would be a pity if anyone were put off meditating or stopped their practice if they took too much notice of the slightly harsh and military attitude that some teachers have.

To meditate is, in fact, to enter a friendly ocean of consciousness.

Summary

So we have this wonderful spectrum in meditation, from the agony to the ecstasy. The agony comes from observing and breathing through our resistance, learning to be truly present to our wounds and to the unreality of our daily personalities. It hurts to remove the layers of habit and protection. It hurts to be honest with ourselves. The ecstasy begins with the profound relaxation and nurture that happens as thoughts, feelings and body move into a harmonic silence. In the midst of this we hold our focus. The pain returns perhaps as we find ourselves breathing through the general nature of suffering upon our planet. The ecstasy manifests again as our consciousness begins to catch the harmonics of the cosmos and we keep breathing through the bliss.

INDIVIDUAL MEDITATION

2. First Principles

My purpose is to simplify the many different approaches to meditation, and to make them understandable and accessible. It seems to me that they all include certain distinct and identifiable features. I list the six features now briefly and then deal with them one by one in greater detail.

CENTERING

ALIGNMENT   REVIEW

the
meditator

EXPANSION   AWARENESS

SERVICE

The six features are:

Centering. Relaxing, calming and coming to a point of inner quiet.

Alignment. Attunement to and exploration of our inner self.

Review. A review of our psychological state and our attitudes and actions since the last meditation.

Expansion. To expand our consciousness and explore the dimensions of 'inner' and 'outer' space.

Awareness. To become aware of and attuned to the various aspects of our environment — immediate, personal, local and global.

Service. Through the use of attunement, prayer and invocation to draw in and radiate a helpful atmosphere and energy— love and healing — to wherever it is needed.

Although I say that meditation contains those six features, they do not necessarily occur in neat and separate boxes of consciousness. Consciousness dances like an ocean, having its own tides, storms and currents. In some meditations, all six may happen in the same wave of consciousness. At other points in time, however, one feature only may be dominant for a while. For example, we might go through an extended period in which we are mainly focused on self-review and self-healing. At another time, our major focus might be aligning with our inner self. While during yet another rhythm of our lives, our main focus might be on compassion and blessing.

Very generally, it is possible to say that there are cycles of dynamic creativity followed by periods of reflection. One of these cycles of creativity followed by reflection might last half an hour; or it might last several years.

Is It Real?

I suggest that the basic structure of meditation involves Centering, Alignment, Review, Expansion, Awareness and Service. All this, however, says nothing to the beginner about the new psychological dimension in which it all takes place. It would be useful therefore to look at how we perceive and understand what happens in meditation.

Meditators and psychologists talk a lot about consciousness and expanding consciousness. Active meditators talk a lot about the impressions, insights and education they receive in meditation. But, to put it bluntly, if we are sitting there eyes shut and silent, how on earth do we know that what is happening is real? Perhaps it is just our brain cells throwing up a world of fantasy. Perhaps the whole business is an intricate illusion.

This is a problem that faces all people who do inner work. It raises important issues concerning discrimination and judgment. But let us be clear in the first place that, sitting silently and watchfully, we certainly do receive impressions that are valuable and insightful. It is possible, of course, that they are created by our imagination, but it is also possible that they come from what the Yoga Sutras of Patanjali call the 'raincloud of knowable things.'

In meditation, particularly as we expand our consciousness and stretch our awareness, we begin to acquire new information and impressions about ourselves, about life and existence. But how exactly is this information perceived and known by us? It sometimes comes in pictures and sounds, because that is the way that the mind-brain of some people interprets and registers the information. But for most of us it comes in a form of direct knowing or intuition. We just sense and feel it, and know it.

My own understanding of this sense — a sense which I

use and trust all the time — is that our physical bodies are intricate energy fields which can register other energies and atmospheres. This energy field, or aura, then anchors the information into our nervous system and then is *interpreted* into conscious knowing by our brain and mind. It is this process of interpretation, however, that requires careful monitoring. Our interpretation of an atmosphere or quality felt by our energy field will be affected by our own unconscious dynamics and projections, and may therefore produce false perceptions in meditation.

So working with this sixth sense requires watchful discrimination. It is important to understand the fallibility of the process of interpretation in each of us and to recognise clearly that our psychological state and history may determine, or at least colour, our perceptions. This is not an overwhelming difficulty providing we remember to be observer to everything, including the most startling insights or 'messages.' There is no need for us, as observers, to be cold and serious. The fat Buddha smiles warmly at the illusory nature of human life.

So we may receive visions, insights and realisations. All the way through meditation, we are poised, receptive and focussed. Our whole attitude is intuitive and attentive to different atmospheres and impressions. For some people meditation, from beginning to end, is an intuitive dance as realisations and insights filter through into consciousness.

There is, though, a core experience of meditation which is not open to misinterpretation. This is the sense of peace that comes through the whole body. Have you ever drunk a warm drink and noticed as the warmth moved through you? The peace and awareness of meditation are like that. It is subtle but also very obvious, like a change in room temperature. When you feel this deep peace, then you are in the flow, the tao, of meditation, connected with the harmonics of the universe. Notice this experience. Let it all the way in to your self and your body. Value it.

Also, when our consciousness expands, this is an experience we cannot misinterpret. In some of the esoteric Buddhist teachings or the writings of Ken Wilber in the west, there are attempts to describe the different stages and experiences of consciousness expansion, but I am not going to attempt it in this book. It is a very mental exercise and open to egoism unless carefully discussed with a peer group. These expansions of consciousness happen naturally and gracefully to everyone. Some of them are subtle and some are very powerful. Just feel blessed when they do come and have some slight caution because psychological depression often follows as part of the process of integration.

The greatest allies of discrimination, knowing what is real and true, are time and patience. Through the passage of time, the excitement and illusory nature of any perceptions will fall away, and you will be left with a *wise* impression of what seems to be useful and true. What is wise will stay with us.

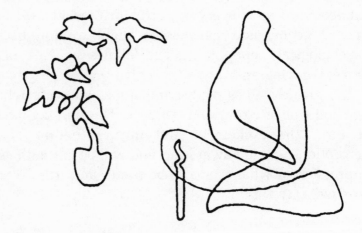

Sitting in a simple home-made environment

3. Location and Beginning

The Space

The experienced meditator can meditate anywhere and under almost any conditions, but it is much easier if we have a place that is quiet and undisturbed. We need, therefore, to find a quiet spot in our home. It is helpful, if possible, always to use the same place, for over a period of time it will build up an atmosphere which is helpful to your meditation; but it is not crucial.

It is pleasant to set aside a particular area in the home and to give it particular attention; to keep it especially clean and to always have fresh flowers there, and to light a candle there before you begin your silence. All of this can also help place us in the right frame of mind. Moreover, a small cared for meditation area in our home can enhance its whole atmosphere. You may, however, choose to do your daily meditation somewhere else such as in the park or in a local church.

Many people with families feel embarrassed, overwhelmed or intimidated by them, and feel that it will be impossible to meditate at home and be left in peace and not made fun of. My suggestion is that folk in this situation have no choice but to call their family together and to explain the challenge. I have worked with many people, especially women, who are cautious about openly talking to their families. Some have found it helpful to hear how they might begin such a conversation: *I wish to explore this new hobby and interest. It is meditation. I need to be able to sit undisturbed for 20-30 minutes a day. It is important to me because ... I think the best room will be ... Does this work for you? I think the best time will be ... Does this work? May I have your support? I need it.* If your family will not support you in this inner work, then I am not at all certain what to advise, other than to suggest that you notice the general family dynamic around you and seek some strategy to help change it.

The people with almost insurmountable practical problems are single parents with young children. Single parents are often so stretched that to create a regular time for meditation is an inappropriate strain, for what they need is nurture and TLC. If as a single parent you feel strongly drawn to meditation, then I suggest that the easiest strategy is to bring a meditative consciousness into things that you are already doing. Remember that meditation is relaxation, focus and breathing — and, as such, does not necessarily have to be done sitting in silence. Some parents I know do it during particular household tasks or when out walking in the park.

When my own son, James, was little and I was also regularly looking after other children, I would often go into a meditative focus when he and the others were sitting on or around me. In fact, he got so accustomed to me meditating that often if he found me meditating, he would simply come and sit snugly into my lap. This stopped as he got older. Around the age of three, he would come and whisper in my ear, 'Is your bottom relaxed?' A smile and gently ignoring him worked to hold my space, but I realise I was lucky. There is a story about a meditator who lived alone in the forests and trained a bear to brush away the insects as he meditated. One day there was a fly which would not go away. The bear, wanting to serve his master, picked up a piece of wood and smashed it down on the fly. But in killing the fly, the bear also cracked the meditator's skull. I have never been certain of the inner meaning of this story, but am reminded of it as I think of the children.

Time and Timing

Meditation needs to be practised daily. Without silence being taken daily, there is little if any chance at all of meditation becoming effective. It needs to be anchored in regular and disciplined practice so that it becomes part of our basic biological rhythms as a human creature, so that our often uncooperative personality not only accepts it, but also actively looks forward to it. Certainly, meditation cannot be approached in a casual or haphazard manner for this will guarantee failure.

Again we have this strange paradox. We are moving into a realm of deep relaxation and flowing consciousness, but we will not be able to achieve it unless we have the discipline to sit daily. The paradox is the balance and relationship of relaxation with discipline.

Starting a practice requires sincerity and a calm and adult commitment. We have to make a clear and conscious decision about what we are doing.

The minimum of time that needs to be taken daily is twenty minutes. It does not matter particularly when we do it. Different people have different rhythms. Nor do I think it crucial that we sit at the same time every day. The only thing that is crucial is that it happens every day.

There are, however, a couple of points that may help us choose the timing. The first is that it is not helpful or comfortable to meditate shortly after we have eaten. A break of at least an hour is needed. The second is that it is not easy to meditate when we are tired, so choose a time when you feel relatively alert.

As I wrote in the first chapter, beginning a practice is not easy as the personality resists the new discipline and the threat of transformation. To begin with the sitting may prove difficult, uncomfortable, frustrating and irritating — but this is normal. There are some people who have the good grace to move immediately and easily into the flow, but most of us have a harder time. We need to be patient and to realise that we are introducing our inexperienced and rebellious personality to a new psychic rhythm. After a while everything will calm and the personality will actively expect and want its periods of silence. It is helpful to be aware, though, that even experienced meditators experience periods of irritability and unease. This is part of the human condition as we put forward resistance to working through behaviour patterns and attitudinal patterns that arise to be changed.

My suggestion is that beginners give themselves at least twelve weeks to begin to get into a rhythm. You have to give yourself a good chance to begin to taste the dancing consciousness of silence. It is very subtle and does not come like a sledge-hammer thwacking cosmic awareness into our brain cells. It is subtle and gentle, like the stroke of a butterfly's wing. Imagine how silent we need to be to notice and appreciate the stroke of the butterfly wing. Imagine how good it is for us to be that silent, receptive and attentive. Simply to be quiet is good for us and good for those around us.

Some people, no matter how long they give themselves, continue to find it impossible to enter the atmosphere of meditation and for these people it is very helpful to meditate in a class or with a group. Not only does the group atmosphere help one's first attempts, but the social atmosphere can help to comfort one through the early difficulties. It is very difficult to find a group that will be of no help. You cannot go wrong if you choose a Buddhist group. (Look around in your local library, health store or alternative bookshop for notices of local meditation groups. There are also two correspondence schools I recommend at the back of this book.) Many people also find the

Transcendental Meditation movement a helpful beginning as they go through early difficulties.

Be assured, though, that these early difficulties will pass as, in the symbolism of the *Bhagavad Ghita*, we saddle, harness and tame our mounts.

4. Centering

Relaxed and Aware

Meditation can only happen if our physical body, emotions and mind are quiet. There are many schools of yoga, and many different breathing and concentration exercises, whose purpose is to achieve this quiet. These physical yoga or concentration exercises can be particularly helpful in our life generally — for physical health, for instance, or for a more disciplined attitude to work. Familiarity with these techniques is not, however, essential in order to move successfully into meditation.

People are very close to meditating when they are daydreaming or in a state of contemplation. To be contemplative is to be relaxed and to be gently considering this or that or nothing. It happens sitting in an armchair smoking a pipe; or watching television and taking nothing in; or in the bath; or the classroom; or lying in a meadow.

Meditation is to be in the same physical and psychological atmosphere as contemplation — relaxed, unworried, calm — but *at the same time* to be totally alert, to have flicked on an electric switch of *awareness*. It is to say in our mind, 'I am conscious, alert and self-aware.' We are calm, unworried, uninvolved and relaxed. Yet in the midst of this calm one is fully awake. This requires a clear mental focus which comes from practice. It might most usefully be called *effortless awareness*.

Body Posture, Body Language and Relaxation

It is important that the body is comfortable, but at the same time it is helpful if the spine is straight. We can sit cross-legged on the floor or sit normally in a chair (this is known as the Egyptian position). It does not matter if the spine is supported or not; it only matters that the spine is straight, but not strained. Some people are able to meditate successfully lying down, but very few and I therefore hesitate to recommend it. The face needs to look straight ahead and its expression be calm and serene.

This might all sound too regimented, but the reason for this focus on posture and on facial expression is the link which exists between body language and mood. If, for example, you grimace and clench your fists for a while, you can sense your body moving into a mood of frustrated anger. Equally, if you relax your shoulders and smile, you will begin to feel friendly and full of goodwill. Body posture reflects and aids our inner state and mood.

Sitting upright...

The straight back evokes and demonstrates that we are awake and alert, not psychic slouches. A calm and if possible beatific facial expression reflects and evokes a helpful mood. There are many religious sculptures and paintings whose figures demonstrate a facial expression which we can usefully copy. I am thinking particularly of some portraits of the Madonna and some sculptures of the smiling Buddha.

So we straighten our spines and put on a beautiful expression — no matter what our mood. We start to breathe calmly and come to focus. This, incidentally, is a wonderful strategy for achieving self-control in many situations.

Relaxation and Breath

It is crucially important and often very difficult for the beginner to be physically relaxed.

Meditation schools teach various methods, the most usual of which is to relax the body area by area. You begin with the toes, then the feet, then the ankles and so on upwards. In my experience it is possible to short-cut this method by focusing on two particular areas: the *solar plexus* and the *face*. If we can get these two areas relaxed, then the rest of the body seems to follow. Some of you may have other crucial physical areas, but I find that the solar plexus and face work for most people.

The actual act of relaxation is done with an effortless form of will. One of the wonderful attributes of human beings is our ability, at will, to change our mood and attitude. This works for relaxing the body. Shut your eyes and begin to relax the face muscles. Stretch your mouth if you need to. Don't forget around the eyes and forehead. To calm a tense solar plexus may be more difficult and we need to be more patient and gentle, calmly allowing any tension to dissolve.

Many schools teach breathing exercises which can be

usefully used to take us into calm. These exercises always
have a particular rhythm. The most well-known breathing
rhythm, found in cultures all over the world is the rhythm
of 7—1—7—1 . . . A count of seven on the in-breath, pause
for a count of one, a count of seven on the out-breath, pause
again for a count of one, a count of seven on the in-breath
and so on. The other very well-known rhythm is one in
which there is no counting, but the exhalation flows
effortlessly into the inhalation, which in turn flows
effortlessly into the exhalation, and so on. This rhythm is
perfectly smooth with no pause or break of any kind between
in-breath and out-breath. It is well worth practising these
rhythms so that they can be easily used when needed in
meditation. Classes in Hatha Yoga are very helpful.

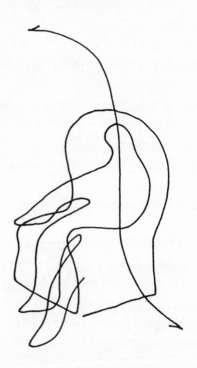

Relaxed but self-aware

Very effective and quite sufficient for beginning most meditations is simply to count one hundred breaths. *One,* breathe in. *Two,* breathe out. *Three,* breathe in ... and so on. If you are not calm by the end of counting to one hundred, you can simply continue to count another one hundred breaths. If you are still not quiet, you may continue to count further. Sometimes I count up to three hundred before I begin to feel calm. I did have one student who could not count beyond twelve without losing her focus and drifting off. We talked about her difficulty. She then came to understand that the concentration skill needed to count her breaths was exactly the same skill required to hold her ordinary focus of awareness in meditation. She then found the motivation to achieve the necessary concentration.

It may seem very frustrating and even a waste of time to spend so much time counting. If it does feel frustrating or a waste of time, then you can be certain that you have the wrong attitude in the first place. It is precisely the internal sense of impatience which needs relaxing. If it seems that nothing will work, then the only thing to do is to simply tell yourself: *I am sitting here for the next half hour doing nothing but counting and that is just fine.* We need to say this to ourself with a firm but philosophical and humorous attitude, aware of the actual poignancy of the difficulty. The personality does not wish to be quiet and brought under the control of calm. Be certain, though, that only to count our breaths for half an hour is a piece of work well done and that at the next session, or the one after, you will enter into a state of calm.

Relaxation is a matter of attitude and purpose: we must actively want to do it. The paradox again: we must be actively motivated to be passive; effort to become effortless.

As we count our breaths, some people are helped by thinking peaceful thoughts and deliberately conjuring up serene images: landscapes, people, animals, plants, places we love.

If the diaphragm or chest continues to feel tense, it is very helpful to take a few deep breaths to help release the tension. The most effective way of pulling air deep down into our diaphragms is to *exhale* as far as we can, in fact exhale until it even begins to hurt. Then let the air rush in. Try it. It is a surprising effect if you have not done it before.

We need also to be aware of the natural nervous energy that we all carry and any ongoing physical discomfort or resistance to meditation may, in fact, signify that we need exercise. It is a clear message from our bodies that we have physical tension that needs to be worked out. Some folk dance or stretch before sitting. Others give themselves a good long shake.

Grounding, Earthing, Being Fully Present in Our Bodies

Over the years that I have taught and practised meditation, the importance of grounding the energies of the body and the psyche has become increasingly clear. Ninety-five per cent of people who fall asleep or daydream in meditation do so because they are not grounded. Equally those few people who experience some fear and anxiety in meditation need to ground.

The technique for earthing is basically very simple and there are several variations. Essentially we need to imagine and sense the energy of our body going down beyond our feet and deep into the earth. Some people imagine a flow of energy down the spine going down to the centre of the Earth. Others sense themselves as being a tree, with the spine as the trunk and with deep roots into the earth. If you are in a very spaced-out state, then it is useful to sense energy roots going down from every part of the body including the solar plexus, heart, forehead and crown of the head deep down into the earth.

The reason that all this works is because our consciousness has a tendency, when we are either relaxed or threatened, to slip out of our body. When we go into meditation we have to relax our bodies and personalities, and this sends us subconscious body signals which we normally associate with going to sleep. Equally, when threatened and anxious — in this case either by the new sensations of meditation or by the threat of having to look at parts of ourself we would rather ignore — our adrenalin begins to flow and there is a natural reaction of *flight*; in this case the flight of our consciousness out of our body.

Being earthed keeps our energy and consciousness present in our bodies. This is also very important if we have a mystic inclination and our consciousness is expanding out into realms of grace and bliss. Most of us have met spiritually inspired folk whose heads are in the clouds, but whose personalities are very unintegrated. Earthing is what is needed. Combined with careful attention to the breath, it keeps us fully present and allows whatever new awarenesses or fields of consciousness we meet in meditation to ground and integrate in our bodies and personalities.

The most attractive image of a meditator who is fully grounded is the pot-bellied smiling Buddha, sitting fully on the Earth. For those of you familiar with the concepts of eastern martial arts or Tai Chi, this smiling Buddha has his Chi or physical vitality anchored firmly in his lower abdomen. I often advise space cadets who have a genuine problem with grounding themselves to do an introductory course to a martial art or Tai Chi. In a few weeks the most ungrounded folk will learn how to be present in their bodies.

And this surely is an essence of meditation: to unfold into new consciousness, but also to be present here and now.

Centering the Mind

The human mind is complex and energetic. In the same way that the physical body and emotions need to be relaxed and calm in order to meditate, the mind also needs to be relaxed. This does not necessarily mean that it needs to be absolutely silent, but it does have to be on a low or mellow enough volume so that we can come to center and be observer to our minds. Again, we have to remember that we need to observe our mental activity, especially when it is impatient or judgemental about our meditation process. For comfortable meditation I have noticed that some people need the mind to be absolutely quiet, whilst others can meditate while it burbles quietly on.

An essential part of the centering process is to get the mind mellow enough that we feel comfortable. In my own process I only need to count my breaths and focusing on my counting and on my breath is enough for it to calm. The essence here is an attitude of patience. If we have an attitude of patience, that is already most of the battle won to relax the mind. In some schools particular phrases or prayers known as mantrams are taught. In other schools students are given images or patterns known as mandalas. Holding a clear focus on the mantram or mandala brings the mind to calm and to focus.

Silencing the Endless Chattering Mind

Many meditators, occasionally or often, suffer from an endless babbling commentary kept up by their minds. No matter how long the meditator waits, the mind simply will not go quiet. Some meditators simply ignore the mind's chatter and get on with meditation, and can be a detached observer to the active mind. Other meditators, however, need to silence the it. There are several approaches to this problem which are useful:

1. *Mantrams.* A mantram, almost any mantram, can be repeated very fast or with great intent over a period of time, from a minute to half an hour. This can both drown out the psycho-babble and display to yourself that you have the discipline and attitude to beat it. A prayer that is meaningful to you repeated with sincerity over and over again can also silence the babble.

2. *A Trick.* This is a silly trick, but it quite often works: Suggest to the mind, or order it, to babble on in a foreign language. As we do not understand everything it is then saying, it is not so easy to be distracted and we can get on with meditation. The essence of this exercise is that it creates a space of detachment between our inner meditating self and the chattering mind.

3. *Self-reflection.* It is also, of course, possible and sometimes useful to use the chattering mind as an opportunity to reflect upon what it is about our life and psyche that anyway produces this chattering. There are several possibilities:

The first is simply that you are a novice at meditation and have not yet learnt how to focus and concentrate. Continuous and sustained practice of meditation without dropping the daily rhythm will always eventually bring about focus. Also, there are many books which give concentration exercises which can be very useful. (See, for example, Mouni Sadhu's *Concentration.*)

Second, the chattering mind may simply reflect the fact that you generally lack self-discipline and focus in your life. How one copes with that realisation is up to each individual. Usually the answer includes an act of will and clear decisiveness; and again the use of concentration exercises may prove useful.

Third, the endless chattering mind may, in fact, not be a problem but a *message* to you that you have a problem or anxiety which is being ignored and which needs attention. In this case it is best to have an attitude of patient and interested compassion towards the state you are in. What is the source of the stress or the anxiety? Have I been aware of it all day? What attention and what nurture do I need to give to myself? In the next section, I will deal in more detail with personality review, but it may reassure you to recognise that at certain times it is appropriate to let the whole of a meditation focus upon your problems and anxieties. It may sometimes be appropriate simply to listen to the chattering mind for a full twenty minutes. Who knows what has been repressed and requires care and attention? We should allow to surface in our consciousness whatever needs to be noticed and cared for.

Fourth and finally, the endless chattering mind may simply be reflective of the kind of cultural life we generally lead, in which the mind and intellect are prized to the point of excluding the human attributes of natural instinct, beautiful action and intuition.

Centered, relaxed, calm and observant, we can proceed to align with the core self.

5. Alignment

Awareness of the Core Self

When we are first learning meditation or when we are physically or psychologically exhausted, it may be enough simply to enjoy being centered and relaxed. Just to take twenty deliberate minutes of calm can be immensely valuable as its effect gently spills over into the rest of our life. Certainly, whenever it seems appropriate to use meditation just for getting calm, we should do so without any sense of laziness or evasion. Life is often difficult and I think that we should take comfort and nurture whenever we need to. Meditation simply as relaxation can be perfect.

Relaxation is, of course, only the first step in meditation. The calm of relaxation and being centered can then be deepened into an attunement with our inner self. But what exactly does attunement with one's inner self mean? There is a difficulty here in describing the inner psychology of human beings in a language that is universally acceptable. In all religions and teachings of spiritual philosophy, however, and increasingly in modern approaches to psychology, there is the realisation that human consciousness is not simply what appears on the surface of the complex human personality. Behind the everyday personality is an inner identity.

This inner identity is complex and profound—so complex that one psychologist called it the 'multidimensional personality.' In other times it has been called the 'psyche.' The multidimensional personality is not simply an area of consciousness that is to do with everyday human life. It also possesses a dimension which transcends everyday experiences. When we touch and come into contact with this aspect of our psyches, we touch a dimension whose major feature is an expansive and unconditional love-wisdom. When we touch this dimension it is experienced in various forms: profound peace, bliss, unity with the universe, silent knowing.

Alignment is to bring ourself into closer harmony and contact with this inner self. Instead of this inner self hovering distantly in our awareness, we can deliberately enter into a fuller relationship with our soul. The Vipassana tradition would say, and in a sense rightly, that true inner consciousness will come present anyway over time. Other traditions, however give encouragement and helpful techniques for working towards a closer resonance.

There are various degrees and stages of alignment with the inner self and meditation by meditation the degree of alignment changes. When we first begin to meditate we rarely enter fully into awareness or experience of the core self. It is enough simply to bring ourself into harmony and resonance with it. Later, after months or perhaps years, we may enter gracefully its full awareness. Every individual has her or his own private inner path to tread in making this relationship with their real self. The experience and the nature of increasing alignment are unique to each person, for everyone has a unique history, unique growth patterns and a unique set of lessons to be learned.

This may all sound rather unclear, but unless we are in the middle of an experience of ecstasy or bliss, our experience of the core self is very subtle. It is not, however, so subtle as to be completely illusive or invisible. A metaphor I often use is that the soul is like a feather and the human personality is like a bowl of water with this feather floating on its surface. Once the personality is quiet and we are focused, open and alert, then we can become aware of a different texture in our consciousness and being. It is more than the experience of relaxation. It has a certain nurture and satisfaction about it. Its natural resonance is wise and accepting. It feels good. This is the first experience in meditation of the atmosphere and true quality of the core self. It feels beautiful and it is linked in this beauty to all life. A phrase I often use to describe it is *mellow nurture*. It is because of this ongoing experience that so many people spend so much time in meditation.

I often mention the business of irritation and resistance. The experienced meditator has irritation and the mellow nurture of the inner self *simultaneously*. In fact this is the experience of much meditation and is the core of the transformative process.

Again, it is useful to use the analogy of being a good host in the void our psyche. Be aware of the core self. Invite it in. Notice, no matter how subtle, its presence and build up a relationship with it. Its presence over time will become more powerful. This is the work of a lifetime.

Switching on the Light

The gentle and patient approach of simply waiting and observing may, for some people, be a perfect practice for a whole lifetime, but there are also more active approaches.

In all schools of meditation that teach techniques there is unanimity on the necessity for consciousness to be firmly located between and behind the eyes. This is the location of the pineal gland, sometimes known as the third eye, and it is thought that this is the place in the physical brain where the core self anchors, in self-consciousness, into the human body. In some traditions this location in the brain is beautifully called the 'throne of the soul.'

The major method of aligning oneself is by an act of

spiritual aspiration. With will and concentration we place and hold our focus behind our eyes. We hold it there and we are aware, observant, effortlessly watchful.

We need to be continually aware that to enter into good meditation is not to lose consciousness in a mystical sea of calm, but to be astonishingly and calmly aware. This light of self-awareness can be switched on gently and slowly, or quite sharply and deliberately. And indeed, over time the light of self-awareness expands as we experience more expansive dimensions.

When our consciousness is focused behind our eyes, the screen at which we look is blank. Any images, like thoughts, need to be watched with detachment and allowed to calm. Like our thoughts, we must not be fascinated and distracted by these images. We may learn something from observing them and recognising that they are superficial images of underlying realities. Beautiful images are often a distraction thrown up by a resistant personality. I once led a group in which a man was overwhelmed by a vision of a Being in white offering him a gift. We spoke about it and he realised that his lesson was not the image itself, but his excitement and glamorisation of it. He needed to learn about his subconscious need to boost his ego with exciting experiences. Then, more sober, he began to smile wryly. This class was happening in a conference room in a hotel and before the class he had had a cup of tea in the restaurant, where he was served by a waiter dressed in white: the Being in white offering him a gift.

The Essential Technique

Calm and centered — remember your solar plexus and face muscles are relaxed — and with a detached sense of good humour, you need to bring your consciousness to a focus within your head and a few inches behind your eyes. It

should seem as if you are looking out at a black scr
with our consciousness effortlessly focused here
vast majority of meditation work is done. All meditation
schools without exception work from this physical point.
Why from this particular place? Again, because it is that
part of the brain which, it is taught, actually anchors and
works with impressions from the inner self.

Over the years, you may sense your point of focus
moving temporarily to other places within your head, for
example above the crown. Many people find that for a while
their focus sits naturally in their heart. Sooner or later
though it will return to a few inches behind the forehead.

Experienced meditators, who live in an attuned way,
enter into alignment at the same time that they center. Sitting in
the right posture and gently calming ourself can be enough
to allow us to come into alignment and to become focused
in our head and behind our eyes. When we are just beginning
the practice of meditation, we may often find ourself reaching

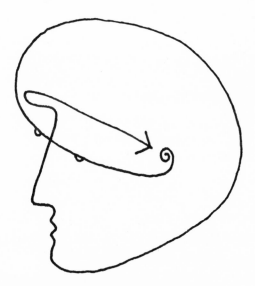

Focused behind our eyes and forehead

alignment, holding it for a moment and then slipping from it. This may cause some frustration or distress, but do not worry; over time and with practice, you will be able to reach and easily hold alignment. There are, of course, various techniques which can aid the process.

These techniques only work when they are built on top of a fundamental psychological attitude. What is crucial in alignment is the willingness to be detached from our everyday personality. We need to have an attitude of distance from the identity we present to the world every day and which we may carelessly accept as the only reality. This mantram is useful:

I have a body, but I am not my body.
I have emotions, but I am not my emotions.
I have a mind, but I am not my mind.
I have a personality, but I am not my personality.

There now follow particular exercises and techniques which help bring about alignment. Always remember, though, that you must always be relaxed and calm, and that your intention is to bring yourself to a detached point of focus behind the forehead — and to hold it easily.

OM and Other Mantrams

A mantram is a sound, a word, or a group of words, which when repeated sufficiently puts the person who is saying them in touch with the atmosphere which the word represents. This effect is achieved partly through suggestion and association. For instance, repeat the word *beauty* sufficiently — *beauty ... beauty ... beauty...* — and it will work subconsciously to put you in touch with the essence, meaning and experience of the word beauty.

A mantram also works through the essential resonance and harmonic of the sound itself. Some sounds, for example, are harsh whereas others are soothing. Hebrew and Sanscrit are languages in which each consonant and vowel has a special resonance and meaning. Hebrew and Sanscrit sacred words, therefore, not only represent some mystical or sacred thing, but their actual resonance and sound work with tone and vibration to touch certain atmospheres and qualities.

The most well-known and easily effective mantram is the Sanscrit sacred word OM or AUM. The two pronunciations are interchangeable according to one's personal intuition as to which is appropriate at a particular time. (AUM has a note to it which, it seems to me, is slightly more earthed than OM.)

OM has no exact translation, but it can be explained thus: It is divided into three parts.

First, there is the very beginning of the vowel outbreath, the first moment of the word's expression before even a sound is heard — this represents the thought behind and the very beginning of all creation.

Second, there is the long continuation of the vowel sound which represents the breath of creation moving through space in order to manifest the divine thought.

Third, there is the vibration of the consonant which represents the breath vibrating into form life and the manifestation of the divine idea.

Like all mantrams the OM can either be sounded out silently in the imagination or aloud. Ideally in private meditation, mantrams are sounded silently. It should be sounded as many times as feels comfortable. If beginning meditation, try sounding the OM five or six times. Sound it out sincerely and with confidence. Then relax. Be focused in the head and experience any changes that the mantram may have brought about. If no inner change of atmosphere is experienced, sound it out again several times. It may even be necessary to continue sounding it for several minutes. Stay relaxed all the time. Let the OM do its work. Finally the meditator will experience its effect. The *Yoga Sutras of Patanjali*, which I recommend as the best description of the mystical process available, states:

'Through the sounding of the Word AUM and through reflection upon its meaning, the Way is found.

From this comes the realisation of the Inner Self and the removal of all obstacles.'

Other mantrams can be made up particularly to suit one's needs. For example, something as simple as: 'I am centered and aligned.' Or, 'In my head I am authority in control.' Or, 'All is Peace.' Each of these statements is a clear affirmation of the state of being in alignment. It is useful, then, when sitting in the mellow nurture of alignment to see if there are words that express your experience. These words can then, at a future date, be used as a mantram to help you back into that space.

Each individual meditator can intuit and make up the mantram which best suits them for the needs of the moment. Repetition and clear intention are the keys to the success of a mantram as they bring us into resonance and harmony with the statement's intention and inner meaning.

Mantrams have been described as the basic tools in the technology of meditation. Some meditation schools and teachers initiate their students into mantrams which resonate in such a way as to put the student in touch with some transcendent or transpersonal energy or being. This can sometimes be very useful. Students, however, usually go on to experience meditation in a much wider context beyond the mantrams of their particular school. But every individual, of course, must intuit their own private path.

(NOTE: *Transcendental Meditation.* This is a quick note for those many people who trained originally in TM and want to investigate the ideas of this book, but are anxious lest the techniques are incompatible. First, there is no incompatibility. The trick is to hold on to the deep sense of peace that you receive from using your mantram. Hold on to the experience of peace but gently release the mantram. Get accustomed to the vibration without the mantram; and then go on to experiment with these other approaches.)

The Perfect Being in the Heart Exercise

This is one of the most famous exercises for bringing about alignment. It is very simple and also has a very beneficent general effect on the meditator.

Perfect being in the heart exercise (after Jacobello del Fiore, Venice, 1439)

Having achieved physical relaxation and calm, imagine a person or being who, for you, is a symbol of spiritual perfection. This may be a well known religious figure or it may be a figure who is totally private and known only to you. In your imagination get a clear sense of this being; this sense does not need to be a technicolor picture. Sense what the being looks like and also the beautiful and perfect atmosphere which it radiates. Contemplate its qualities. Then place this being in your heart. Contemplate it in your heart. Sense, experience and flow along with its effects.

Again, remember to keep your body erect and elegant, and the expression on your face calm and serene. Over time this exercise will bring you, via your heart, into clear alignment.

Climbing the Planes

This is a classic and extremely useful exercise that serves several purposes. It is based on the assumption that there are dimensions of life and existence beyond those dimensions perceived by the usual five senses. This assumption is at the core of *all* meditation traditions, but there are, as yet, no scientific instruments sufficiently sensitive to register these dimensions. In the western meditation tradition, these other dimensions are frequently called 'planes' and they are mapped as being one on top of the other.

The most dense plane is that of physical matter.

Next there is liquid.

Then there is air.

Beyond that there is a dimension or plane which can be seen by many people as the silver electric shimmer around trees.

There are then more semi-physical, or 'etheric,' planes which are related to dimensions akin to physical electricity and which, for instance, conduct light, sound, and other known phenomena.

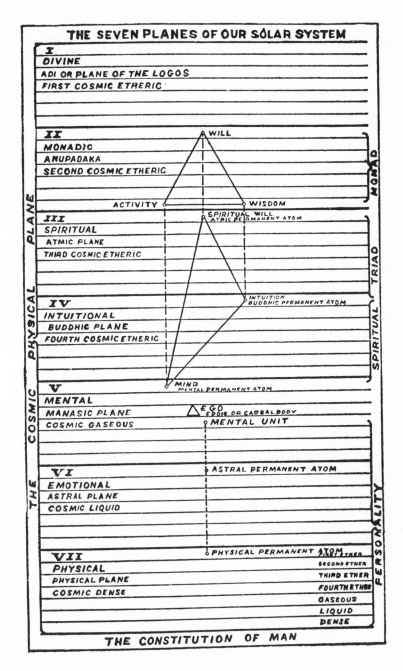

The planes (from A.A. Bailey, Letters on Occult Meditation)

Then there are those planes and fields of existence which we experience as emotion and feeling. There are different qualities of emotion, some more dense and heavy than others: 'heavy' emotional vibrations and lighter 'good' vibrations.

Beyond these emotional dimensions, we begin to enter the realm of thought and mentality; again there are different qualities of thought, some heavy, some light — lower mind, higher mind. As one rises through these mental planes one moves into an area that feels transcendent and perfect.

Beyond the mental realm are planes that we experience as intuitive and then as pure spirit.

The diagram from *Letters on Occult Meditation* is a map of these planes. It works in groups of seven — like the seven colours of the rainbow, the seven notes of the octave, and the seven columns in the periodic table of chemistry. If, however, you do not resonate with working with sevens, it is possible to adjust the map to suit your own worldview.

The actual alignment exercise is very simple. Having centered and moved into a state of calm, focus on the first and most dense dimension, that of physical matter. Take a few seconds, thirty seconds at the most, to tune into it and to experience the quality of physical matter. Then raise your attention to the next plane, that of liquid. Again, tune into it and experience its quality. Then, tune into air and experience its quality. Then begin to move up the other planes, stopping and attuning to each one, experiencing its particular quality. Go up the planes/dimensions as high as you can. The essence of the exercise is to: *Experience in your consciousness the quality of each plane and then move on.*

This exercise not only works to help alignment, but also begins the voyage of discovering and investigating inner space and those dimensions beyond our everyday identity. It is an exercise that can also be used after you are aligned,

The planes/dimensions interpenetrate

in order to explore the quality of other dimensions.

If used daily for several years, this exercise also sharpens up the skill to discriminate about the quality and nature of insights and information we may acquire in meditation. For example, if we receive a particular impression, we can then judge what plane it belongs to. It can make a lot of difference, for example, if we sense that some insight or vision is from the higher mental planes rather than the emotional.

In reality, of course, the planes interpenetrate — as Marko Pogacnik's illustration suggests — and do not sit one on top of each other.

Invocation

The techniques suggested later in the book for invoking and radiating helpful atmospheres are also very useful for achieving alignment. As we reach up within our consciousness to touch pure sources of helpful atmosphere, we naturally come into alignment.

Uncertainty

The result of these different types of exercises is to achieve alignment and focus after we have gone into silence. Some people beginning meditation say that they are afraid that they will not be able to recognise when they are aligned. If uncertain, you need only ask yourself: Am I calm and focused in my head behind my eyes? Am I silently self-aware? Am I relaxed and effortlessly present?

When first beginning meditation, you will slip in and out of alignment; you will not be able to hold it for as long as you want. This is quite normal and you should not let it bother you. Over time and with increased practice, you will achieve a satisfying rhythm of self-control. Once you have achieved and can hold alignment, you may hold it for any period of time that feels suitable. Just stay silent and be aware of yourself.

Again, the *Yoga Sutras of Patanjali* has a helpful comment:
'The attainment of the state of spiritual consciousness is rapid for those whose will is intensely alive.

Those who employ the will likewise differ, for its use may be intense, moderate or gentle. In respect to the attainment of true spiritual consciousness there is yet another way.

By intense devotion to Ishvara, knowledge of Ishvara is gained.

This Ishvara is the Soul, untouched by limitation, free from karma and desire . . .

The obstacles to soul cognition are wrong body posture, mental inertia, wrong questioning, carelessness, laziness, lack of dispassion, erroneous perception, inability to achieve concentration, failure to hold the meditative attitude when achieved.'

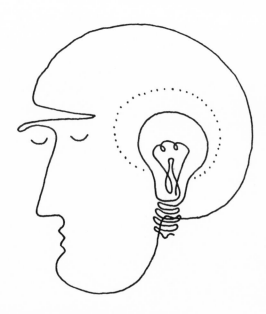

Switch on your head-light

6. Review

I Confess

Meditation is inevitably about self-transformation. Holding a regular rhythm of calm and expanding consciousness introduces a factor into our lives that changes us. The knee-jerk reactions, the habits and patterns useful for survival and for comfort, begin to melt away as we increasingly allow and accept the experience of our core self and meditative awareness.

This whole process can be accelerated and helped along by definite exercises designed to review who we are and what we are doing, designed to look at and change actual attitudes and patterns of behaviour. It is, in fact, a classic exercise of many traditions, but particularly the western meditation tradition, to spend a while every day reviewing our behaviour over the previous twenty-four hours or since the last meditation.

The object of this aspect of meditation is to come to a compassionate and insightful understanding of our own faults and uncreative behaviour patterns. Having understood and accepted them, we can then move into more creative and appropriate rhythms.

The basic format of the exercise is very simple. Relaxed, centered and aligned, we take our mind back over the previous twenty-four hours and slowly go through what has happened to us. This is not a concentration game to see how much can be remembered. Its purpose is to bring into clear conscious awareness our dissonant attitudes and behaviour. Those moments and moods are quite obvious:

short-temperedness, greed, envy, untruth, selfishness, coldness, general moodiness, apathy, inertia and so on.

When we first begin this exercise it is sufficient just to bring this bad behaviour into clear awareness. There should be no judgement or depression. We need, however, to be completely honest with ourself. In this part of our meditation there should be no delusion or ducking responsibility for our actions. This exercise requires an attitude which accepts complete responsibility for who we are and what we do. It is normally very easy to argue that outside circumstances are responsible for moods and attitudes. Sitting alone in silence, however, we have no choice but to take full responsibility for everything that is within our personal experience. This exercise requires detached honesty.

Simply having the courage and wisdom to be honest with ourselves about our bad behaviour is often enough to lead us into a better pattern. There are, however, exercises we can do in meditation which bring a deeper understanding of bad behaviour patterns and help the introduction of new ones. Indeed in *Autobiography of a Yogi*, Yogananda suggests that one meditation is worth a year of living. This is not simply because, through spiritual aspiration, we can accelerate expansion of consciousness. It is due to the fact that in meditation we can re-enact and work through many of the psychological knots which may be preventing, hindering or hurting growth. The key to success in these exercises is honesty and sincerity. We do them alone in the privacy of our silence. They are very personal and do not need to be shared with anyone.

Clearing the Desk

Over the years I have found it invaluable to start my meditation by reviewing myself and my life. I count to a hundred. I feel myself moving into a relaxed and centered space, and I begin to observe my thoughts and feelings. I allow everything to surface. I notice the worries and anxieties, and the pleasures and desires. I provide a lot of welcoming space in the great void of my psyche — again, the benign host to quirky guests — to everything going on in me.

As well as noticing my errors and egoisms, I allow myself time to observe and contemplate particular concerns that may be worrying me, such as troubles in the family, a meeting with a bank manager, planning and relationship troubles at work. I deliberately scan these areas and look them squarely and fairly in the face. If I am nervous about a meeting, then I acknowledge it to myself and do not repress or deny it. This gives me much healing and greater freedom in my everyday life.

I call this part of meditation *clearing my desk*. I allow myself between five and twenty minutes to do this work. It has particular benefits: as well as transforming and healing anxieties, it also gives my busy mind time to have its say. I then go on with other aspects of my meditation. Talking about clearing my desk in meditation classes there are invariably great sighs of relief from students. *I always do that. I thought it wasn't allowed. I thought that wasn't 'proper' meditation. I didn't know I could use my mind in meditation.*

The only real challenge with this practice may happen if you do not know when to bring it to an end or if your mind continues to ramble on. A firm focus and a commitment to other aspects of your meditation should make the transition easy.

Any issues that evoke genuine physical feelings of anxiety during this review need to be breathed through, observed and contemplated. The rules are always the same: stay relaxed, focused and breathing.

I feel fine about allowing myself up to twenty minutes for clearing my desk for two reasons. First, I meditate usually for about an hour so I feel no time pressure. Second, it is an incredibly creative time for me during which I have insights and understandings that save me a great deal of time outside my meditation. In fact, I am happy to regard this time spent clearing my desk as a crucial part of my normal working day. It also integrates my meditation with my social and work activities.

There now follow some basic exercises and suggestions which supplement the essential review and which can be adjusted to suit your particular needs.

1. Thank You for the Lesson

Aligned in meditation, spine straight, stomach relaxed and face serene, remember an incident that angered or irritated you. It is sometimes helpful to choose the kind of incident which continually recurs and causes irritation.

Then visualise the person who triggers the anger. (Again, a word on visualisation. By 'visualisation' I do not mean a clear visual image. I mean a *sense* of the person. This may be partly visual, but is mainly atmospheric and usually quite subtle.) Then imagine yourself kneeling in front of this person and saying: 'Thank you for the lesson.' Let your imagination play with the scenario.

Do it in sincerity. You are thanking the individual for helping you to bring into clear awareness a psychological pattern which requires understanding and healing; but you and you alone are responsible for its origins and now for its healing. You invoked the other person and the aggravating situation into your life in order to let this lesson surface.

There is great grace in this exercise for it releases the other person from any vicious psychological circle in which we are projecting our own inner problems on to her or him. It is based in a mature attitude and the realisation that each of us, and each of us alone, has no choice but to take responsibility, without equivocation or mental reservation of any kind, for ourself. This requires courage and daring.

Performing this exercise you may experience some discomfort and some pain. It is not unusual to cry. This is natural. Be compassionate to yourself. The whole exercise is a most intense form of eating humble pie. The pain and hurt arises because the energy and atmosphere of our inner self is actually changing the energy and atmosphere of our everyday personality. It is a fact of human life on this planet that change takes places through a process of inner friction, as Love-Wisdom vibrates against patterns of psychological materialism — and, through ' friction,' changes them.

Take some time after this exercise, and after all these exercises, gently to assess how you feel. Always be patient and relaxed. From an attitude of inner detachment watch yourself.

2. Electric Love Your Enemy

In this exercise we focus upon someone we do not like.

Bring your hands together in a praying position and place them next to your chest. Now clearly visualise the person and all that you do not like about her/him. Imagine that there is a cosmic source of pure love and that you are in touch with this source which flows into you. Like laser beams, this love shoots from your heart and from your face directly at the image of the person. This love shoots with amazing electric force from you into and around the person, and at the same time, you mentally sound out at quite a high pitch (a high 'A' for musicians) the phrase *I love you!* Repeat the phrase over and over again directly at your enemy. Let the love energy whizz through you for at least a minute.

Repeat the exercise as often as you feel appropriate. It works very effectively to cut through insecure, cowardly or mistaken personal attitudes to other people. As always, relax after the exercise and gently review new feelings.

This exercise can be supplemented by another exercise in which you look for and greet the beautiful inner self which everyone possesses. This exercise can, of course, be carried out into your every day life.

3. Experience the New You + Affirmations

Select any situation in which you experience discomfort and wrong attitudes.

Look carefully at the situation in a detached manner and imagine how you would prefer to behave in that situation. Now imagine yourself actually behaving in that situation in the way that you want. Do not let the experience be simply one that is happening in your imagination, but experience it in your whole body. If, for example, you feel that you should be a more tolerant person, then experience tolerance in your whole personality and psyche.

This can be supplemented by the use of mantrams which affirm and reinforce how it is that we know we should be. The basic technique here is to experience yourself fully in the state that you do not like and then to clearly sound out from within it the mantram that affirms the new you. You might, for example, recognise a disturbing trait of impatience. So in meditation contemplate your impatience and begin genuinely to experience yourself as that impatient person. Then contemplate what it is like to be patient and begin to put the new experience into words. You may not get the words right first time, but essentially it is the intent which is important. In the meditation, then remember yourself as impatient and sound out from within it, fully experiencing a new reality, a mantram like *Like the ocean of infinity, I am Complete Patience*. This kind of exercise can help immediately or may have to be used over a long period of time. After a while it may not be necessary to fully acknowledge and experience the fault we want to transform. It is enough just to affirm the mantram.

If we are continually indecisive in certain situations, we might compose:*I am Fire and Strength; I am Intelligent Will.* Or if we are short-tempered and mean with our partner, *Irritation melts and I am Generous Peace.* These self-created mantrams and affirmations should always work in the *present tense* and never be expressed in the future as 'I will.' In a sense these affirmations and their experience work as a form of self-hypnosis. They anchor the new way of acting into the subconscious and positively help draw one into the new pattern. But do not be too intense or self-serious about all this. As with all other aspects of meditation work, be detached and wise. Remember, the new you will one day give way to a yet wiser and newer you which in turn will also have to change.

Also, you may experience some discomfort and hurt as the old pattern and attitude give way to the emergent you. Be calm, be patient with yourself. You may experience some anxiety doing this exercise. The moment you experience anxiety, consciously relax and breath into it. If you cannot relax, withdraw from the exercise and give the anxiety some analytical or compassionate attention. There may, however, be times when you feel that it is appropriate simply to dismiss the anxiety and to tell it to 'shut up.' This will occur when you recognise the anxiety as part of a habit of self-pity. The self-pity, of course, requires analysis and clarity, but sometimes simply requires that it be fed no attention or energy.

It seems appropriate also to drop in here a piece of advice I learned from a woman friend who had been celibate for several years. I asked her what she did when she felt lustful. She told me what her teacher had said about *desire* generally:

Notice desire — but do not wallow in it.
Put in other words: some patterns need to be noticed but not
given any energy. This is a matter of discrimination and
decision-making. It is crucially important that nothing is
repressed. It is also crucial that we do not waste time
examining something that, in fact, is better ignored. We do
not, for instance, spend hours ruminating on why we have
an active need to breathe. It is part of the human condition.

4. Listen and Talk to Your Problems

It is possible to use meditation to gain profound and useful
insights into both our own psychology and the psychology
of others. This is possible because we often have a deep
intuitive understanding of a situation, but this understanding is blocked from manifesting in everyday
consciousness. Meditation, however, allows a more open
and less repressed flow of information.

The basic technique is very simple. You visualise, or
sense, that person or aspect of yourself that you want to
understand. You then ask it directly to explain itself. You
then let your imagination flow with the explanation that is
given.

The trick is to not block the flow of intuitive information
that comes to you — just let it flow. You can assess the
information afterwards, but while it is emerging and coming
to you you should be open to its psychological validity. At
some level it has meaningful reality. How you integrate it,
though, is a matter of calm and wise intelligence

For example: Bring into your consciousness an individual
whose behaviour or motivation towards you do not
understand. Think perhaps of someone who appears to
react negatively, aggressively, or fearfully towards you.
Clearly sense this person before you. Now, in your
imagination, ask this person why he or she behaves like this

towards you. Let your imagination flow with what the person answers. The exercise allows one's intuitive understanding and insight to surface.

It can also be applied to one's own attitudes and behaviour. There may be a certain kind of situation in which you always behave negatively or aggressively—and you do not understand why. In precisely the same way as above, you can ask yourself why you behave that way. You the observer talks to you the everyday personality and listens to its answer.

A very useful technique here is to understand that our mind and emotions and physical body are each capable of speaking independently. You can address questions separately to your mind or emotions or physical body. *Tell me, emotions, why do I behave like this?* Listen to yourself gently and carefully.

Sub-personalities emerging from one psyche/personality

You can, for instance, also ask your body questions about diet. Or what your emotions need generally to achieve tranquillity. This simple technique of listening to yourself can be carefully used to care for and to heal yourself.

I believe that being one's own therapist is one of the most powerful aspects of contemporary meditation. It combines the power of Vipassana — being present to our suffering and breathing into and through it — with the power of modern counselling and therapeutic techniques. I advise all my students to acquire the skills of Vipassana. I also advise all my students to become familiar, in some way, with the skills of dialogue in modern counselling and therapy. This can be done either by being a client in counselling or therapy, or actually training in counselling or therapy. There are also a few very useful books which give a taste of therapeutic dialogue. (See the *Booklist*.)

Listen to yourself - be aware of healing

5. Heal the Past

It may be that when you ask why you behave in a certain way, you will come to a deeper understanding of things from the past which have hurt and wounded. It is possible in meditation to go some way to healing these wounds.

Very gently, from a focus of detached alignment, remember the situation in which you were hurt. With care and with courage let yourself enter again into the experience of that occasion. Be aware of how it hurt and how it scarred you. Do not hold back on entering fully into the memory for this exercise only works if we have the courage to re-experience the pain. This requires sincerity and also a certain carefully used sense of the dramatic.

As you fully re-live and experience the hurt, realise that you are of course also watching yourself. You are a dual being.

Now cradle yourself with an attitude of compassion and love, and let that love enter and reach the very centre of the memory and of the pain. Begin a process of healing. Forgive and understand the actors in the situation who hurt you. We may even thank them for the lesson.

Continuity

With all these exercises that we do during the process of review, it is important not to look for instant changes and transformations (although there may be some), and to remember that we have embarked on a life-long process. These kinds of exercise and the whole education of knowing ourselves will continue on a daily basis throughout our whole lives and beyond.

7. Expansion of Consciousness

One of the most exciting aspects of meditation is the opportunity it provides for deliberately expanding our consciousness, for reaching out to experience and to be inspired by new dimensions.

This expansion of consciousness has two arenas in which we can operate, the personal and the cosmic. We can expand our awareness to know increasingly subtle dimensions of our own psyche and we can expand it also to know increasingly subtle dimensions of the cosmos. The two areas of expansion are intimately interlinked.

A Caution Against Straining or Forcing

Before suggesting specific exercises, it is important to sound out a gentle note of caution. Under no circumstances should any meditation exercise be forced or strained. Force and strain in meditation are a symptom of unhelpful impatience, of spiritual ambition, and serve no constructive purpose. They lead only to nervous exhaustion. At a practical level, trying to force an expansion of awareness is anyway never effective.

True growth and change occur when our meditational life is reflected in an everyday personality life of greater service and harmony. In a vibrational and very real sense, it is only when our outer everyday personality is vibrating with the new rhythms of a more harmonious way of living and service that we can actually hold on to and anchor properly a new expansion of consciousness. Otherwise our personality vibration grates against the inner consciousness we are attempting to hold and prevents it integrating effectively. Moreover, in a moral sense, meditation is meaningless unless it is integrated in our everyday behaviour. In general, meditational progress has to go hand in hand with more generous and less egoistic daily behaviour.

This caution about never forcing an expansion of consciousness, however, should not in any way interfere with one-pointed concentration of purpose, dynamic aspiration or the point of tension that we sometimes need in order to achieve a new state of consciousness.

All of this may sound over-cautious or patronising, but some folk on the mystic path have a tendency towards imbalance and intensity — I know it in myself — and I do not want to encourage it.

Expansion Within

The expansion of our consciousness fully to embrace our inner self and transcendent nature is a subtle and delicate affair. Indeed it resembles a love affair, the greatest romance possible. The quality of each individual's romance is unique, but there are certain inner features we all share.

Before we can begin to explore our inner self, it is helpful to have some kind of a map or a blueprint to guide the journey. We already have the basics of such a map in the notion that we are dual beings: there is an outer personality and an inner self. When we center and we align we bring ourselves into connection with our inner self. The meditation then has a texture of mellow and nurturing calm which is the foundation for anything else that happens. This texture is the basic experience of our core self and it is the plateau of consciousness from which all true meditation takes place.

I want now to make some general statements about how we experience the core self, but I do not want them to be taken dogmatically. We each have our own way and I am just outlining general tendencies. The energy field of the

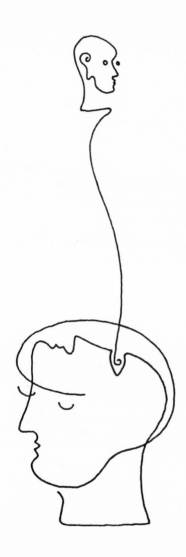

Reaching up, peaking and hitting a new plateau of consciousness

core self is all around us and permeates every cell and fibre of our body — but most of the time we do not feel or notice it. In general the energy of the soul anchors most strongly into us through our heart and through the crown of the head.

In the *Perfect Being in the Heart* exercise two chapters back we imagine a perfect being sitting in our heart and we focus our attention there for a while. This is a way of bringing us more fully into the resonance of our own soul. When we are able effortlessly to hold this point of contemplation, it is very interesting to move on to another exercise and to give this heart-glow some extra attention. Pose some questions. What is the source of this glow? How far does it extend? What does it tell me about myself? Can I turn up the volume on its radiation? In the silence see what answers emerge through your subconscious to consciousness.

The other area through which we can stretch our consciousness more fully into the dynamic of the inner self is the crown of the head. This is the area directly above the center of our head. This really needs to be done very gently. Begin with simply focusing your awareness a few inches above the center of your head and see how long you can comfortably hold it. Carefully try this out for a while, always making sure you are grounded and always breathing. You may begin to feel anxious, you may feel strange sensations and hints of a new consciousness. Stay calm and let the new experience come down fully into the whole of your body using your breath. One of the inner laws of meditation is: *Whatever frightens or excites you is something you will have to get used to.* Getting accustomed to something new in our consciousness can only be done through consistent calm, earthing and breathing.

The Long-Term Sequence and Peak Experiences

There is a general sequence to consciousness expansion and growing awareness of the inner self which it would be useful to describe here. (It might also be useful here to refer back to the map-diagrams of the inner planes on pages 51 and 53.) The process which I am describing is one that occurs over many years of meditation:

(a) When we start our meditation practice, it may seem as if we have to hold the personality perfectly still in order for the distant resonance of the inner self to be felt.

(b) As time passes and as we begin to enter a natural meditation rhythm, the distance between the silenced personality and the inner self decreases. The texture of our meditation becomes mellow and sweet. Now, many people, before they *permanently* achieve this ongoing mellow texture of the core self, receive a *hint* or *taste* of it. It comes tantalisingly through, like the early raindrops before a shower, and may be experienced over just a few seconds; or over several minutes. In comparison to normal consciousness, in comparison to the usual atmosphere, it will obviously feel wonderful. It may feel ecstatic and blissful. Then, to many folk's dismay, it does not return at the next meditation. Please understand that this is not a one-off taste of divinity, sent to tantalise you, but it is a genuine precursor of a state of consciousness which will one day be normal for you.

It is also good to realise that all the way through our meditation 'career' we will receive tastes of new states of consciousness, which we will only fully achieve in the due process of time. I have been caught several times in the disappointment and self-disempowerment that comes from not recognising these tastes as signposts, but expecting to enter immediately and fully into the new consciousness.

You can imagine, can't you, that if someone has been a manic and anxious speed-freak all their lives that the first taste of inner peace, experienced only for a few seconds perhaps, will seem like a divine revelation. Over a year or so, holding to daily meditation, that person will eventually achieve inner peace as a normal flow of meditation. Other people may slip more easily into inner peace.

What I want to underline — in this context of consciousness expansion — is that the 'peak' experience, in this case that of inner peace, is a peak that later becomes a plateau where we sit naturally and effortlessly. All peak experiences, in the context of meditation and spiritual transformation, are steps towards a new plateau of consciousness.

(c) In meditation, sooner or later, we have an experience of a new type of consciousness. In fact, for many us, each meditation brings a gradual unfoldment. These experiences may be dramatic or they may be subtle. The point is to recognise them and understand that our next step is to bring our consciousness fully into this experience and to become wisely accustomed to it. Naive excitement and thrilling to the experience is only a temporary state — to be enjoyed and savoured and then to be transcended. The purpose is to bring our consciousness regularly and easily on to this plateau — for this new plateau now becomes our normal meditative condition. You then experience a true change in consciousness and recognise that you truly are your inner self.

(d) To help this process along it is useful to spend some time letting your awareness feel out into the aura and electromagnetic field above and beyond your head. It is also useful to integrate the new consciousness into the whole of your body, particularly the base of the spine, the stomach, the heart and the throat. Experience the new awareness in all the cells in your body, toe nails to hair on your head. (You may perhaps drop in here an exercise from the previous section and speak with and listen to parts of your body.)

(e) This plateau of consciousness you have achieved is a space from which to now enter yet a higher consciousness. After a time, you will catch the sense of an elusive new peak of consciousness to be aspired to and achieved — a new plateau of greater love and more subtle and higher vibrations. Your consciousness must now reach up and expand to reach this new peak. Always gently, always hand in hand with better personality behaviour, you will sense how to move into the new change. I cannot give instructions here because how these expansions happen is specific and unique to each individual. The core self has its own guidance systems and these will depend on your own particular state, history and potential.

(f) From each new plateau, yet another peak of consciousness will appear.

This cycle is the wonderful expansive nature of meditation throughout our lives.

Expansion out to the Cosmos

It is also helpful and natural to expand our awareness out into the cosmos, both geographically and in terms of consciousness. The purpose of this is to aid our inner expansion, to become generally more sensitive and to acquire what might be called cosmic ecological awareness.

Before using any of the exercises that follow, another gentle note of caution: When doing them do not be over-impressed by any images your receive. Stay observer to any images, intuitions or sensations you receive. If something is really true and useful, it will remain meaningful to you over a long period of time. A wonderful aspect of these exercises is the freedom it gives us to explore all kinds of issues and questions of metaphysics without anyone peering over our

shoulder or telling us what to think. Using the approach
and techniques of these exercises, you can explore anything
in the cosmos that evokes your natural curiosity.

1. The Inner Being of the Sun

This exercise works with the Sun. There are various levels
to it. The first stage, silent and aligned, is to become aware
of the Sun. Any impression of heat or light finds its source
in the Sun. As you can tangibly feel and sense the Sun,
become aware of how close it really is. The distance in miles
is meaningless. Let your imagination flow into the sun and
experience its fire.

The second part of this exercise is more subtle. First of all
tune into the fact that you are a multidimensional soul, an
inner self, incarnate in a personality and dense physical
body. Then become aware of the idea that the burning
physical body of the Sun is also just the body of an inner
being. Tune into the nature of the inner being of the Sun.
Many traditions suggest a relationship between the core
self of the Sun and the star Sirius. How does this inner being
radiate through the whole solar system? The oldest known
prayer, the Sanskrit *The Gayatri*, addresses this being:

> *O Thou Who givest sustenance to the universe,*
> *From Whom all things proceed*
> *To Whom all things return,*
> *Unveil to us the face of the true Spiritual Sun*
> *Hidden by a disc of golden Light*
> *That we may know the Truth*
> *And do our whole duty*
> *As we journey to Thy sacred feet.*

You can experiment with sensing the blessing of this inner spiritual Sun flowing down through your head, down through the core of your body and blessing your whole being. It can then radiate outwards.

2. Attune to the Essence

In the cosmos, according to the experience of many people, there are archetypes and pure sources of the most beautiful and interesting energies that we can know and experience. This exercise consists in reaching out with the greatest sensitivity of our awareness to touch and experience these pure sources. For example, contemplate the meaning of Love in every day life. Then contemplate its meaning for the whole planet and then beyond. What is Love on a cosmic scale? What does Love mean within our whole solar system within our galaxy? Tune in at these different levels. See how sensitive you can be. Be attentive to the subtleties you pick up. Gently expand with the experience.

You can, of course, explore other qualities in the same way: Divine Power, Light, Spiritual Direction, Healing, Grace, the Cosmic Christ. How much can your consciousness touch?

Reach out and be open to impression.

3. Cosmic Geography

It is also possible to explore the cosmos *geographically* in your mind's eye. You can begin by letting your imagination travel around the Earth. Become aware of the vast expanse of oceans and the size of the continents. Imagine beams of light going out from your body circling the Earth and returning to you. Now sense outwards towards the Moon. Circle the Moon and then reach out to the Sun. Become aware of the other planets. Recognise that our solar system is but part of a galaxy, the Milky Way. Move your imagination around the galaxy and become familiar with its other stars and constellations. Move beyond our galaxy and see how far your imagination can reach.

Especially as you work with this kind of exercise, always stay anchored.

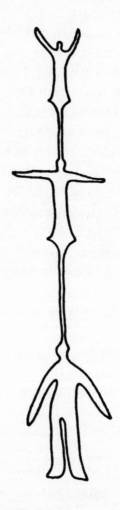

Expansion of consciousness to touch planets, sun, stars

4. The Full Moons and the Zodiac

This is an exercise that runs in cycles of 28 days and which uses the full moon cycle to explore the energies and atmospheres of the different signs of the Zodiac. It is particularly appropriate for people interested in astrology.

Towards each full moon, begin to tune into the Zodiacal sign that the sun is in at that time. For example, when the full moon occurs between January 21 and February 21, tune into the zodiacal sign of Aquarius. For forty-eight hours leading into the full moon, gently tune yourself into the right zodiacal sign. Contemplate its symbols and become familiar with its meanings It is also quite helpful to use some Sanskrit mantrams. The mantram for Aquarius, for example, is, *Water of life am I, poured forth for thirsty Men*. For Virgo, *I am the Mother and the Child. I God, I matter am.* (All twelve mantrams are given in the Appendix.) Gently repeat the mantram to yourself and contemplate what it might mean at different levels of reality — personal, planetary, cosmic.

Universality

All religions and systems of meditation contain prayers and exercises which are tools to expand consciousness and divine awareness. If you find that you enjoy this kind of meditation, then it is worth browsing through the many hundreds of books available on meditation. It is possible also that the greatest inspiration will come from less obvious books on subjects like astronomy, astrology and cosmology. A child's map of the universe may be the perfect stimulus for expansive contemplation. Certainly, the few expansion exercises I have just shared are not meant to be definitive. They are intended to indicate a particular mode and inspire meditators into creating their own particular forms of investigation.

8. Awareness

This aspect of meditation has a very attractive simplicity. Its purpose is to give us a deeper and more sensitive knowledge of our environment; to give us a sense of anchored perspective and to develop compassion. It consists of one extended exercise which you can adapt to suit your time and circumstances. It requires the freedom of a playful imagination in which you just let impressions come to you. Again, it may take a long while for you to feel secure about the accuracy and meaningfulness of your perceptions. In the meantime, be the detached happy observer.

Ecological Awareness

Silent and aligned, bring your attention to focus upon your immediate surroundings.

In what kind of a state is the space in which you are meditating? Is it a mess? What is its atmosphere? What is in this space and what does it need?

There may be plants in the room. What kind of rapport do you have with them? What is their state of health. There may be a room in your home that requires greater care and cleanliness, or a different, more appropriate colour. Ask yourself some questions. What is my attitude to this environment? What do I need to do to enhance it?

Be fully aware of where you are. *Be here now.* Let your focus then expand to include the whole building in which you are meditating. Again, explore its atmosphere, its state and its needs. Move outwards beyond the building into the gardens, landscape or roads. As before, become aware of their atmosphere and needs. Gradually expand your awareness to cover the whole locality.

Your attitude should be one of compassion and caring — from the mind and from the heart. Now let your attention move even further afield across your city and country, across your continent and across the planet as a whole. It is impossible to ignore the incredible natural beauty of the planet. At the same time, it is also impossible to ignore the social injustice, the suffering, the warfare, the poverty, the famine. Let your consciousness focus upon all this and contemplate it. Recognise also the hidden pain and exquisite beauty which exists in every human being on the planet.

Be aware of the other realms, beings and lives — mineral, plant, animal, angelic. Be aware of the Earth as a whole, Gaia. All life, the whole and the parts are interconnected, and all require care.

Awareness and Compassion

Seen from the outside meditation can seem a cold and heartless exercise. The person sits there, eyes closed, impassively breathing. There is also a great deal of talk about detachment and awareness. To someone who does not know, all this can suggest that part of the meditation process is to become cold-hearted. This is not true. We may lose our emotionalism, our devotions and ideologies, but we gain other things. Through meditation we increase our love-wisdom, our sense of purpose, our degree of enlightenment and our compassion. Why is this so? Most traditions teach that this is the nature of the core self which is in resonance with these qualities throughout the universe. Whether that is so or not is for each of us to discover. I have never heard a story though of meditation leading to degeneration, bestiality or other negative patterns. The history and the experience of meditation is very pure.

This general exercise of *awareness*, then, brings to the meditating individual a compassionate sense of the interconnectedness of all life. It also brings the meditator an awareness that all life is in the process of change and transformation. Energetically and through consciousness the meditator is unavoidably and inextricably involved in this total process. Our growth and expansion of awareness is intimately connected with the growth and changes of every other life form — from a single stone through to the planet as a whole.

It is part of this exercise, therefore, to meditate in different environments and to explore the different atmospheres in different places. If you find yourself somewhere which you instinctively sense to be interesting — from a beautiful place in landscape through to an urban slum — then meditate there. This is a way of expanding our relationship with where we actually are. Far from meditation lifting our consciousness away from everyday realities and environments, meditation makes us more present and aware.

In the next section we deal with how we can add practical service to this awareness.

9. Service, Invocation and Radiation

Meditation can be of very practical service. In meditation, we can radiate and channel good and healing energy to where it is needed. This form of service works in two ways: through natural radiation and through deliberate invocation, channelling and radiation.

Natural Radiation

Simply by sitting in silent meditative tranquillity, we radiate calming, loving and healing vibrations. Some people may find it difficult to believe this really happens, but think of all the homes, buildings and gardens where there is a natural atmosphere of peace. Part of the atmosphere may be due to the landscape or harmonics of the architecture, but it has also been created by the people who work, contemplate, meditate and live there. Churches, temples and libraries are wonderful examples of places that hold the vibration of people being silent. Especially where there has been much prayer or meditation there can be a distinct and moving presence.

Everyone can effect their environment in the same way. Simply by sitting quietly, the quality and resonance of the inner self radiates. The meditator feels it first of all in the mellow nurturing silence — but this quality radiates outward. It gets caught, so to speak, in the space between the electrons in the molecules that make up the air around us or in the brickwork of the walls. The material world absorbs the vibration of the meditation. (It also, of course, absorbs the vibrations of our moods.) We can, therefore, tangibly feel the effects of meditation in our homes.

But this meditative radiation also travels further. Its effect, of course, on the world in general is not huge. But when it links up with all the other prayerful and meditative energy it can help to change the world. I say more about this cumulative effect later on in the section on *Networking*. So, when you are meditating, recognise that you are gently and usefully serving. Throughout the ages men and women, alone or in communities of meditation and prayer, have dedicated themselves to this work.

The quality of atmosphere is also enhanced by the fact that the core self is itself in resonance with and receptive to very lovely archetypal energies. Our normal everyday social selves are not, to say the least, normally humming from contact with archetypal sources of unconditional love or

Radiating a beautiful atmosphere to the environment

wisdom or enlightenment or divine purpose. The core self, on the other hand, is humming with this contact. The core self acts like an aerial picking up the more beautiful, higher vibration wavelengths. The apparatus which then receives and radiates the wavelength is the human personality and body.

Whether all this is true or not is something that people either intuitively know or actually experience. Again, one of the more interesting and stimulating joys of meditation is precisely the space and time to explore the reality, or unreality, of these dimensions.

Purposeful Invocation

If we accept and experience these inner dimensions, then it is possible to actively cooperate with them in order to amplify their beneficial effects. In the first place it helps simply to give the whole phenomenon some attention. It is worth taking a few minutes in meditation to contemplate and explore the notion that we are helpfully radiating. In a confused life it may be the only thing we do every day that makes sense and is worthwhile. Just giving it attention gives it more power. You can if you want imagine that you are radioactive and experiment with turning up the power of the radiation.

We can also work with a much more dynamic method. The basic technique is very simple: We reach up in our consciousness to touch the very highest sources of love and healing, of purpose and enlightenment. We then deliberately call down and imagine this energy flowing through us and out to where it is needed. We can do this very gently or we can do it with a powerful compassionate demand on behalf of all life. In the imagining and sensing of it happening, it really happens — following the inner law that energy follows thought. Again, certainty and confidence about what is happening will come with time and experience.

I will now go through a technique of invocation in detail.

A Technique of Invocation

1. From your centered and aligned space in meditation, become aware of your planetary environment and the need all across it for love and healing. Feel the poignancy of it and experience compassion.

2. Imagine that above you, above the crown of your head, there is a source of pure love and healing. The higher that you reach up in your consciousness to it, the greater its purity and power.

3. With all your spiritual aspiration lift your consciousness up as high as it can go to touch this pure source of love and healing. As you reach up, be aware that you are doing so on behalf of all life on the planet and that you have the right to ask for and to invoke that the energy of love and healing flows down. You will experience an inner point of tension as you reach and hold the peak.

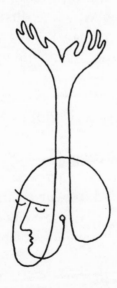

Reaching up to touch a pure source of love for invocation

4. Hold this peak for as long as you can—this will usually last between thirty seconds and five minutes.

5. When you feel that your contact is slipping, relax gently and let the energy subside.

6. After a minute or so, you may feel it appropriate to reach up once again to that pure source and repeat the process. The rhythm varies from situation to situation, but is similar to waves on the ocean. If you feel it is right to reach up again, then do it — and again hold it for as long as is comfortable before once more subsiding.

7. Having released the tension for a few seconds, imagine the energy flowing down through you. Let this period last as long as feels appropriate.

8. And now imagine the energy flowing outwards from you and being distributed to where it is needed.

9. Finally, if you want, sound out the OM the vibration of which will ensure that all is distributed.

OM OM OM distribution of energy

To repeat, the general format is very simple:
1. Be aware of what needs help.
2. Reach up to contact and invoke the energy source of Love.
3. Relax and let it flow
4. Make sure all the energy is distributed.

There are certain prayers and invocations which can be usefully used to facilitate this whole process of invocation and examples of them are given in the *Appendix*.

It is often quite a useful rhythm to do the reaching up three times in all. It is also possible to call down three different types of energy on each peak: the first peak can be for Light — which brings enlightenment and illumination; the second peak can be for Clarity of Spiritual Purpose — the kind of energy which only allows the beautiful and loving; and the third peak can touch Pure Love.

The Least We Can Do

Sometimes this form of service will be the major feature of your meditations. Sometimes it will not be so significant. You will feel for yourself when it is appropriate. It is important, I feel, that every meditation has a few moments focused on this form of energy service. It is the very least that we can do. It shows whatever else may be happening in our meditations, that at least our hearts are in the right place and we are trying to help. In fact I believe that it is crucial, profound and effective service. Moreover, many meditators have their most transcendent, transformatory and inspiring experiences doing this work of invocative service.

Some years ago I wrote a prayer, called *A Glastonbury Invocation*, that attempts to integrate the way that I work with invocation and which I hope can be used by people with many varying beliefs. It is inspired by the Lord's Prayer and the Great Invocation both of which are in the appendix.

There is a Source of Love which is
the Heart of All Life.
Let that Love flow
Source to Earth
Heart to Heart.

There is a Source of Light which is
the Mind of All Life.
Let that Light flow
Source to Earth
Mind to Mind.

There is a Source of Power which is
the Purpose of All Life.
Let that Power flow
Source to Earth
Purpose to Purpose.

We are that Love
We are that Light
We are that Power.

Peace and Healing on Earth.

Full Moons and invocation

Sensible twentieth-century citizens may react negatively or sceptically to any mention of the full moons, but if superstition can be put aside we can see that we are merely part of an ancient and very effective tradition.

It is particularly useful and effective to use the time of the full moon, every twenty-eight days, as a period of particular focus to invoke love and healing for the planet. This is because there is a magnetic effect at the time of the full moon which aids this kind of inner work. Just as the Moon acts to draw the oceans of the Earth in tides, so at the full moon the vibration of matter, including that of the human brain, is slightly accelerated. When the human brain vibrates faster it is more sensitive and can anchor down inner information more easily. This is the reason for the much reported and scientifically verified phenomenon of greater psychiatric dis-ease during the period of the full moon. The full moon is, therefore, also an opportune time for more intense spiritual work.

Let It Flow

Just a final word in this section. Often, invocation does not need to be focused work. Just sit and be aware of the extraordinarily beautiful energy that can flow through you. Simply reach up to it or simply surrender yourself to it. Be beautiful, be calm and be silent. It will flow.

10. More General Comments and Advice

Simplifying Matters

In the previous chapters I have described different things that we can do in meditation and I am worried that some readers might interpret me in a way that is too mechanical and regimented. My worst case scenario is a meditator, having read this book, allocating specific amounts of time to each phase: five minutes to center, five minutes alignment, three minutes expansion of awareness...

Yes, we have to center. And, yes, it is impossible to enter into deep meditation — that of the mellow nurture — unless we are aligned and sensing our core self. But we need to be comforted by the reality that even the most experienced meditators, as they deal with their stuff, sometimes cannot center or align themselves. Sometimes the intense stimulation of everyday life and psychological stimulation, from inner and outer causes, overwhelm the silence. This is a signal to look at the conduct of our whole lives.

Beyond centering and aligning, we can simply stay in the mellow nurturing atmosphere, but always alert and observant, grounded and breathing. We can also move our focus on to one of the other techniques of meditation. I am concerned that when you place your focus upon a particular technique you will do it in a way that is intense, serious and narrow. Once at a very crucial moment in my life, when I was filled with fiery aspiration, I broke down because I was not experiencing what I thought I ought to have been experiencing. The situation was so difficult for me that I wept for a while. I then went back into my inner world and had the experience that I expected. The weeping had released my tension and melted my ambition. Our inner awareness picks up nothing if we are tense or mechanical.

Start with a Seed

There are two easy ways of moving into the techniques. The first is that from our calm state of center and alignment, we observe a particular thought, sensation, idea or intuition that comes into our awareness. Observing it, we intuit that it is appropriate to give it greater attention. This intuition about whether to give it attention is based, however, in some wisdom. The wisdom concerns purpose. We can be very clear about this. If something crops up in meditation we can ask ourself these questions: *Should I give it attention? If I give it attention will it serve how I review myself? Will it serve how I expand my consciousness? How I become more aware? Will it be a blessing for myself, my community or environment?*

If we can answer these questions in a positive way, then we can gently and carefully bring the subject into our full attention. Then we just follow where the flow of our meditation goes — always the conscious observer. This is how I always move from the jumble of thoughts at the beginning of my meditation, through the time that I call 'clearing my desk,' into proper self review. Into what is already happening I place the seed of that which I next want to give my attention

Moving into a new focus, start with a very small seed of an idea and then gradually expand it. For example, if you intuit that it is appropriate to gain some awareness of your heart center, you do *not* conjure up in your mind's eye a big red picture of a heart which overwhelms you. You, instead, gently focus on the idea of your heart center. A small seed of awareness. Just hold your focus on the seed, stay relaxed and open, and then see what you perceive or sense.

If we start with a big dramatic picture then we shall nearly always be dealing purely with a *projection* of our own thoughts. Tuning into the seed, waiting carefully and watching with openness and no expectation, will lead to authentic experience and perception.

The factors of Centering, Aligning, Review, Expansion, Awareness and Invocation have all been laid out in this handbook as distinct and separate aspects of meditation. They are conceptually different and each feature alone could make up the focus of the whole of one's meditation. In practice, however, they merge and dance with each other, reinforcing and helping each other. Sometimes one particular aspect will predominate as that aspect is the most important learning area during that time. Thus, for instance, you may meditate for several weeks with the major focus being upon reviewing yourself. At another time, the major focus may be on expansion. This is fine and part of each person's unique rhythm. Equally, when beginning or during times of stress, it will be enough just to center and relax.

The general structure of Centering, Aligning, Review, Expansion, Awareness and Service can be used as a reference or check list in order to assess what we are doing and to ensure that we are not missing out something important. We do not need to include all aspects it is not comfortable. Meditation needs to flow naturally according to our individual space and needs. Meditation is private and we have the absolute freedom to make private decisions about what we do in it.

Impressions

I want to say a few more words about validating the perceptions we have in meditation. First, it is helpful to remind ourselves that from the perspective of some practitioners all perceptions are illusory, to be ignored and breathed through. If, however, we remain as wise observer to the perception, they may communicate something insightful, stimulating, even wise.

The whole experience of meditation is a very subtle process. We sit centered and aligned in our consciousness. We then gently focus on one particular aspect or another and we receive certain *impressions*. Our consciousness and imagination then work on these impressions. The problem, of course, is in knowing whether to take any notice of a particular impression. Different people receive these impressions in different ways. If our attitude is calm and sincere, and if we are aligned with love and with the very best, then our inner self filters the impressions we receive and they may all be useful. In my meditation it sometimes seems that I am in an ocean of impressions and that this is the nature of life. Anything significant tends to strike a chord all the way through me or to haunt me.

There is a little story you may not know: A would-be meditator spent years searching the globe for the perfect teacher of meditation. Finally the teacher was found and at last the student received the first lesson. After the meditation the student was very excited and said:

'Oh, Teacher, what beauty! I was surrounded by an ocean of golden light filled with wondrous silver flames. I heard a great echoing chime as if ringing through the whole planet. Ah, wonder!'

The great teacher replied:

'Do not worry, my student, these distractions will soon end...'

Often I think that there is only one useful guideline:
Until the very end be prepared to believe that everything you pick up in meditation is meaningless.

If it is meaningful then *the impression will endure* and you will understand it to be useful as part of a longer learning process. What matters in the end is not the brilliance or glamour of our insights, but how our consciousness expands and how we act in better service.

Rest and Mother Earth Nourishment

The self-discipline of daily meditation is essential, but there will be times when it feels appropriate and perhaps even necessary to take a few days or a few weeks rest from meditation. Occasionally, the physical brain and the psyche simply require a breathing space. If you sense this to be the case, then wisely take a rest. Do not be a devotional taskmaster, but treat yourself with love.

Rest and nourish yourself by reaching down into Earth

This need for rest will not happen often, but you will know when you are straining yourself or on overload. It is better gracefully to demonstrate your intelligent adaptability than to adhere to a temporarily uncreative ritual. Have a rest if you need it. Enjoy your rest and nurture yourself.

You can, if you wish, nourish yourself with a very introvert and earthed form of silence. Sit quietly and relax, but do not focus yourself in the head or align. Just relax, let your head drop forward and go deep within. Be aware of the nurturing energy of the Earth. Feel embraced and sustained by it. Relax and be nourished.

Don't Head-Trip

Although most meditation takes place from a focus behind our eyes and in our heads, although our stance is that of observer, we have to be careful that meditation does not become solely a mental exercise. As personalities we have to round out and become balanced — to be and to act from our hearts as much as from our heads. We need to be clear mentally and emotionally. Be certain in your meditation, therefore, to experience yourself as a total human being and not just as someone who is mentally focused and perhaps repressing other aspects of your beingness and psyche. Move your consciousness around your body. Experiment with the *Perfect Being in the Heart* exercise. Try silently sounding out the OM in different areas of your body, perhaps beginning at the base of your spine and working upwards.

The meditation focus in your head should be based in a balanced and well-rounded general personality, losing none of the attributes that come from your heart. It is usually inappropriate, as a personality, to take meditation too seriously even though it may be the most profound activity in your life. Equally, no matter the difficulties in your life, meditation should be a source of joy and inspiration — even if sometimes it is painful or frustrating to touch that point of joy. There is often an irony here: for it takes great patience, self-discipline and often an act of will to *surrender* to the natural beauty of life.

Eyes Open and Walking

You may find it interesting sometimes to practise your meditation with your eyes open. It is usually easiest to center yourself, align and then open your eyes. Stay detached and calm. Feel the changes.

It is also, of course, possible, to do one's whole meditation while walking in a park or the countryside — like a monk or nun circling the cloisters.

Eyes open exercises help to integrate our inner life with our outer life. The two need to be one and not separate.

GROUP MEDITATION

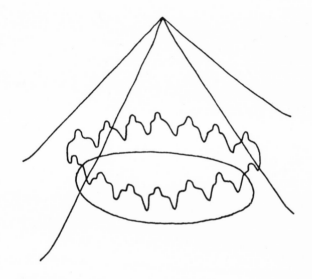

A group meditating together

11. Why Group Meditation?

Group meditation may seem to be a modern phenomenon, but it is not. There have been many communities in the past where women and men have shared silence. These communities have been oases of peace and alignment in fractured societies. In most religious traditions meditation is taught mainly as a group and community practice in the first place.

It may also seem paradoxical that an action, so private and inner, should be done with other people, but working in a group is supportive and helpful.

Group meditation requires a different framework of understanding from individual meditation. In individual meditation we are describing and discussing what happens in one individual's psyche and consciousness. An extreme sceptic, listening to us, could at worst say that everything we describe is just a production, an epiphenomenon, of the human brain and that altered states of consciousness are due to changes in brain electro-chemistry. Individual meditators, supported by the millions who also meditate, know for themselves the truth of the matter.

But to understand group meditation we need to take another metaphysical step beyond the normal framework of the contemporary worldview. For here we are discussing an *invisible* set of connections between people. When people sit in group meditation, their brains are not wired up with one another! Nevertheless the individual meditators share a similar experience which is powerful and beneficial. Meditators share this experience because they are energetically and telepathically connected. We each of us carry an atmosphere, mood, aura, charisma. Call it what you will, it is certainly an energy field which other people can feel.

So, let me be clear for sceptics. In discussing group meditation we are not talking about a social event — a tea party for mystics. We are discussing a powerful energetic dynamic. Just as powerful forces move in observable group dynamics, so they also move invisibly in group meditation. The proof of this can only be found in direct and personal experience.

Over the years my personal experience of group meditation is that it gives me great pleasure and inspiration. I am always fascinated by its texture and atmosphere. I love feeling the tensions subside and the whole group move into relaxation and then alignment. In a world full of tensions, I find sitting safely with a group, sensing the inner dynamics, energising and comforting.

The Social-Psychological Usefulness

Group meditation may not be a tea party, but this is not to deny that the psychological and social aspects of group meditation can be extremely useful. First, if we are starting a practice, or want help sustaining one, then being in a group can provide a very helpful, psychologically supportive framework.

Second, it can be a very powerful *symbolic* gesture. When two people shake hands or smile at each other, beneath the fact of these everyday gestures something meaningful is happening. We are signalling safety and friendship. To close our eyes in a group and to be silent together is an even greater gesture of trust. It allows anxieties, impatience and fear to subside.

Shared silence is a symbolic gesture of anchored spiritual cooperation which transcends egotistical separateness. In fact, many people with an instinct for these realities always take a few moments silence with their colleagues before beginning a piece of work. In modern jargon this is called *attunement* and I shall describe it in greater detail later on.

There is also a more subtle symbolism in attunement and group silence, for it has a levelling effect. No matter the apparent hierarchy or leadership, it melts away in the silence. Individual egos surrender, in spirit, to equality of opportunity. People who have trouble with surrendering to this temporary and minimal gesture of unity, usually have even greater difficulty in surrendering to and experiencing the spiritual unity of all life.

The Invisible Connections

My experience, and the experience of so many others, is that we possess an energy body, or aura, that surrounds us and emanates from us. This information is not new, but has been taught in mystical, esoteric and shamanistic traditions the world over. Our energy field is made up of various types of energy, such as the vital life force that gives us physical health, most often called *prana*. It is also made up of energy generated by our feelings and thoughts, as well as the energy of our inner self. This invisible anatomy is as complex as the structure of our physical bodies.

When we center in meditation, this cauldron of physical, emotional and mental energy calms down. When we align, the atmospheric quality of our inner self is allowed to come in and we begin to feel its mellow nurture. And while all this is going on as a private experience, we are also radiating this atmosphere outwards through our energy bodies into our environment. In group meditation we each of us radiate an atmosphere and we also feel the atmosphere radiated by the others. Our energy bodies experience the changes in vibration and this, in turn, anchors through into our nervous system; it is then interpreted by the brain in a form of direct knowing. This is as tangible as feeling heat or cold.

A clear and everyday example of this is how, if we are connected to someone, we can know instantaneously what mood they are in by just being near them.

Our atmosphere, thoughts and vibrations are picked up and tuned into by others. Because of this some newcomers suffer from an undue nervousness about group meditation because they are worried about the effect that other people will have upon them. This is usually an unfounded fear because people, when meditating, have deliberately moved into a space of silence and purity. But if you are nervous, approach group meditation cautiously and slowly build up your confidence.

The Advantages

Because we radiate and because we can sense the atmosphere created by other folk, it is easy to see how group meditation can be very helpful. There are, in fact, several distinct advantages to meditating in a group.

There is a ripple or wave effect which actually multiplies the beneficial quality. This is similar to the physical effect that can be observed in the ocean when small waves build up to create one large wave. A single individual's calm vibration helps the next person. As that next person calms, their vibration in turn goes back to help the first person. The waves of calm build up. The group as a whole can, therefore, take advantage of the individual or individuals who calm first. Those first individuals create an atmospheric flight-path for everyone else in the group to reach the same state. The combined atmospheric effect of many people sharing silence makes it much easier for beginners to achieve center and alignment as the vibration touches, soothes and aligns them. People often have their first experience of being centered and aligned in a group. One of the interesting features of group meditation is that nearly everyone notices when the whole group has relaxed and come to center. It can also be a great support and refreshing experience for more experienced meditators.

In a similar way, any individual who is reaching peaks of awareness or expansions of consciousness not normally reached by the others in the group, creates an energy funnel which helps the others approach the same space.

These helpful dynamics are referred to in many spiritual traditions. It is, for example, referred to metaphorically in the idea that *when two or more are gathered together in my name...*

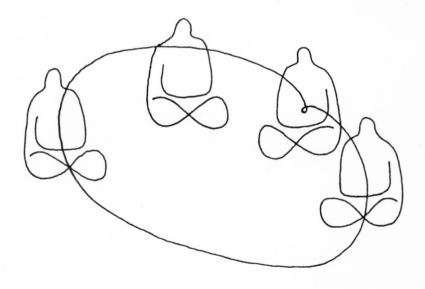

One meditator's calm atmosphere helps all the other meditators in the group

Two Types of Group Meditation

Within this framework, then, we can say very generally that there are two types of group meditation:

1. The first is that in which everybody is meditating individually in their own *separate ways*.

2. The second is that in which everyone is meditating for a *common purpose*.

In the next two chapters I will deal in turn with these two types.

12. Individual Meditation in Groups

In individual private meditation, sitting in silence, we allow ourselves to become aware of the texture and consciousness of our inner selves. This is a nurturing and transforming experience for us. When I sit with a group I am aware that every individual, in their own private and unique way, is also in the same psychological and spiritual process.

In the same way that I require time to relax, center and align, so a group also has its own rhythm. Sometimes I am so stimulated that it may take me a half hour to center. Sometimes, if I am in enervated crisis, my whole meditation may be a struggle as I breathe through my tension or psychic activity. In a group, however, as the group calms, so I too calm as I am affected by the group atmosphere. Even if there are more nervous wrecks than just me, the group dynamic will still work. I can imagine someone asking, 'but suppose everybody's a raving basket case, what then?' I have indeed experienced groups in which everyone was stressed but even so, on closing eyes and bringing the breath into rhythm, the group has gone into calm. It can be miraculous how fast and easy center is reached. It is the exact opposite of group hysteria, as the herding instinct is harnessed here for creative good and for empowering the individual.

This is the beauty of meditating in a group: collective support, but individual empowerment. We share the process of relaxing and aligning. Then, in the support of group alignment, always with that nurturing mellow atmosphere, we can continue with our own private meditation and get on with whatever is there to be breathed through and contemplated.

The texture and sensation of the meditation will be coloured by the group atmosphere. It is sometimes useful and interesting, when centered, gently to become aware of and to explore the nature of the group atmosphere and how it affects us. We can be aware of the helpful energy currents of the other meditators as well as the helpful currents we ourselves radiate. Until you have a good deal of experience in group meditation, I do not think that it is a good idea for you to try purposefully to affect the group atmosphere. If your presence is meant to facilitate a change, then patiently let it happen. If, however, you do have experience then invisible cooperation can be very useful; I will discuss this more fully later.

Even if there is no explicit purpose to a group meditation, there are powerful implicit benefits. We have already discussed the benefits to the individual, but shared silence is also extraordinarily helpful in helping people to work cooperatively together. Without any fuss, in silence, our personality vibrations blend and become accustomed to each other. If there is personality friction in a group, nothing can work so fast to heal it as sharing silence together.

Even if there is no stated specific purpose to a group meditation, I personally feel that it is appropriate for every group meditation to end with a short period devoted to radiating love and to healing the environment. This can be done silently as a part of everyone's private meditation or it can be led with an appropriate prayer, invocation or mantram.

13. Group Meditation for a Common Purpose

For individual meditation I described several basic modes which I hope were clarifying: to Center, to Align, to Review, to be Aware, to Expand and to Serve. These modes can also be usefully applied to group meditation.

When a group *centers*, the individuals relax and create a calm atmosphere.

When a group *aligns*, the individuals accept the joint resonance from all their core selves. The group also aligns with what may be the common or inner purpose of that group.

A group may also *review* and be self-reflective about its state, the individuals gaining insights about their own roles as well as the group as a whole.

A group may choose to give *awareness* to a particular subject.

A group can also *expand* its consciousness together.

A group can work specifically to radiate a blessing or healing as a form of *service*.

Again, like individual meditation, these different features do not need to be regimented and allocated specific amounts of time. A group does not even need to be formally led into the agreed focus. Before the meditation there can be a simple agreement about the focus and how long the meditation is to last. Sometimes though it is helpful to ring a sweet-sounding bell to begin and end the meditation.

Centering and Aligning a Community or Working Group

As I described earlier, even if there is no explicit purpose to meditating together, there is an immensely useful harmonisation in every group meditation. This harmonisation works to bring unity and cooperativeness to separative personalities. It facilitates attunement to a common purpose and vision. And it accelerates spiritual growth as the sense of at-oneness with the meditating group overspills to evoke an experience of unity with all existence.

Because of all this the great majority of spiritual communities or groups with spiritual awareness have a regular rhythm of group meditation. In fact, to risk sounding unduly certain, I am happy to suggest — along with many others — that it is fundamental to attuned and balanced group or community work that the group meditate regularly together. This is the major tool, or strategy, for ensuring that the personalities of those in the group are harmonised and attuned cooperatively to the inner spiritual purpose of the community. (Some individuals and groups take this work so seriously that when it is not possible for the members to be together physically, they link telepathically and meditate at the same time.) The glory of this process is that it happens in silence and that every individual is completely free to respond and attune in the way that he or she wants. Other than the actual sitting together in silence, there are no ideological or other constraints.

Within these group meditations each individual can pursue their own private meditation, but it is helpful if we also keep a gentle focus, with awareness and receptivity, on the group's purpose. This may lead to some creative examination of the nature of the group and its inner purpose. It may mean that we reach up for the very highest inspiration.

It may lead simply to being very silent and aware. We have to follow the thread which intuitively attracts us.

Many people in group meditation anchor pieces of information about the nature and purpose of the group. Again, it is important to maintain the same attitude that we hold in individual meditation. Keep the bullshit-antennae switched on and don't take any of it seriously. If you are going to share with others what you perceived, then be careful how you communicate. Someone else may have perceived something completely different. I have experienced some very awkward situations where deadly earnest folk are sharing their contradictory perceptions. Perhaps this is why some spiritual communities are completely silent — they have witnessed the deadly conflict of competing spiritual visions.

Again, I think that it is totally appropriate that all these group meditations end with a conscious distribution of the healing energies.

Attunement Before Work

It is worth mentioning at this point the usefulness of any group taking a few moments silence before beginning work — whatever kind of work, physical or mental or spiritual. Usually the group forms an informal circle and simply goes silent for a short while, as short as fifteen seconds, and everyone tunes into the other members and to the work to be done. These few moments can be extraordinarily helpful in building cooperation, as well as facilitating a creative and sensitive attitude to the job.

A few words may be spoken. For example: *Let us bring ourselves fully present.* Or: *Let us be aware of the work we are about to do and do it with love and clarity.* If in doubt, say nought. It may also seem right to hold hands. The custom — I do not know where it came from and I do not think it important — is for the right hand to face up, greeting the sky, and the left hand to face down greeting the earth.

After one workshop with members of the Findhorn Foundation, the group I was working with drew up some helpful guidelines concerning attunement:

1. Attunement is never simply a ritual done out of habit.
2. The focaliser of the attunement always demonstrates:
   (a) Caring for the group;
   (b) Sensitivity to the work to be done.
3. The focaliser therefore:
   (a) Clearly and caringly brings the group together in the here and now;
   (b) Sensitively attunes the group to the work to be done.
4. At the end of the period of work, it is helpful if there is a completion or 'detuning' — a holding of hands, a 'thank you' — or whatever is appropriate.

Techniques for Linking the Group

Most of us, when we begin to understand and have some experience of group meditation, find that we instinctively want to help the process whereby the group calms, centers and aligns. Our basis for being able to help is that after we have sat in many group meditations, we become very familiar with the atmosphere of group calm and alignment. We have much experience of how it should be and we gear our own attitude, energy and atmosphere to achieve it. This is a very instinctive process and will vary from group to group and according to our own state.

The basic sensation is that, while being aware of the interconnectedness of everyone in the group and having a clear feeling of the quality of the atmosphere, we extend our energy and consciousness around the circle. Then, taking full responsibility for co-creating the atmosphere and the level of calm and alignment, we hold our own focus aligned and we also *hold the energy of the group*. Like the fat smiling Buddha we extend our benificence out to hold the atmosphere of the group. We do this from our minds, from our hearts and from our cells.

There are also specific techniques that can be used to help a group cohere and reach alignment. One of the simplest is to focus for a second or so on each individual in the group, to acknowledge their presence and to sense the energy link between you. Do it quickly, smoothly and gently. Sense the individual energies fusing into the energies of one group. Another technique is to visualise and sense the group as forming a chalice. The energies of the people form a chalice into which the atmosphere of mellow nurture will flow. Or you can imagine the group as a circle of fire, each individual a flame. You can choose any image or symbol of unity that seems appropriate to you. Or you can simply sense the group as a circle of love. There are many different ways we can do it.

We can also use mantrams or affirmations. They can be said silently or aloud by the whole group, or by one person aloud on behalf of the group. They can be simple like *We are a circle of love. We open our hearts to each other*. Or they can be more complex, like the two that follow:

We are the workers and the Work.
We are One — with the One That Is.

I am one with my group brothers and sisters
And all that I have is theirs.
May the love which is in my soul
pour forth to them.
May the strength which is in me
lift and aid them.
May the thoughts which my soul creates
reach and encourage them.

Macramé Linking

It is also possible to do the linking and building of group cohesion in a more complex and detailed way. I will give here one example of a very effective technique. My hope here is that all the different examples encourage and trigger you into developing your own approach.

This method is called the Macramé technique because, if we could see it clairvoyantly, the energy patterns resemble those of a macramé weave. The basis of this method is to link with everyone in the circle — first from the heart, then from the forehead and then from the solar plexus (that part of the stomach which cradles a child or hugs a tree.)

The first link is made from your heart to the heart of the person immediately to your left and you then carry on, making the link heart to heart one by one, clockwise, moving around the group.

Having completed the circle at the level of the heart, you then repeat the exercise, this time from the forehead. Again, start with the person immediately on your left, linking with their forehead. Carry on clockwise around the group, making a direct connection with each person separately.

The third circle of linking is made very gently from the emotional love center in the solar plexus. Very gently, with care and love, connect with the solar plexus of the person on your left and continue round the circle. This third connection can facilitate quite a subtle healing and calming of jagged emotions. Some people are cautious about linking at the level of the solar plexus lest it stimulate emotionalism. If done gently and following the connection made at the heart and head level, negative emotionalism is never evoked; in fact, a tranquil cleansing and reassurance occurs.

It is enough just to delicately feel the links being made at each level; no intense visualisation or contact is required. I hope you can imagine that if everyone does this technique the result is very magnetic and useful.

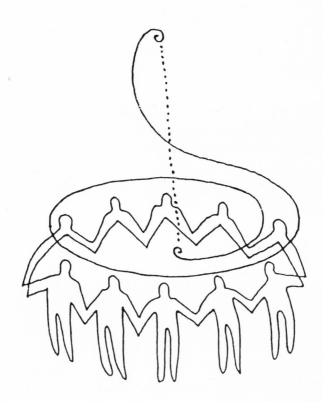

Group members linking with each other

Many experienced meditators also find themselves instinctively balancing the energies of a group or helping to shift what feel like blocks. Here are some examples:

You may notice, for instance, that there is some anxiety in the atmosphere. Your strategy for this might be to earth the group more firmly.

You feel a tension in the solar plexus. You, therefore, breathe into and calm your own solar plexus and connect lovingly with the solar plexuses of everyone else, soothing the group tension.

You may sense a general egoism preventing focus, so you open your heart and put more energy into the group's heart connections.

You might be aware of a dullness, so you send some energy around to connect people's heads and to bring the focus up.

There is one absolutely golden rule in all this work. If you feel any tension, effort or exertion in your body, then immediately stop doing this kind of inner work. This inner work must only be done in the purity of soul alignment and you will recognise this because your own body energies will be calm. Any tension will indicate that you are working with your personality and are, therefore, not only part of the problem but also probably making it worse. If your body feels serene all is well. Any tension, then desist.

14. Leading Group Meditations

To be able to lead a group meditation is a useful skill. Groups often need the clarity of a single voice setting the tone and guiding the sequence. In this way all members can focus on the same aspect or theme at the same time. Leading them and learning to lead them is also very useful for us. It teaches us greater sensitivity. It challenges us in new and interesting ways. It is empowering and confidence-building.

Essentially it is not difficult to lead group meditations. Having taught it for many years, I reckon that people need to have or to develop four qualities:

Sensitivity.

Clarity.

Inner rhythm.

Confidence.

The sensitivity is needed in two essential ways. First, we need to be extremely sensitive to the fact that it is an honour that we are allowed to lead a meditation. And we need to be sensitive to the atmosphere of the group. Our voice and the ideas we speak will be breaking into the sacred space of other people's meditation. Our initial attitude, therefore, needs to be humble — not grovelling or weedy — and careful. The voice has to be carefully pitched. It should be clear, not too loud, and lacking in emotionalism.

Second, we have to be clear about the actual needs of the group and of the moment. Whatever is said must be necessary and appropriate. It must creatively help the group meditation. Whatever is said, there must be a clear reason for saying it. *If in any doubt, do not say anything*. And whatever you do say, keep it short and clear; it has to be understandable. Simply ringing a bell can often be the best way to signal the beginning and end of a meditation.

The sense of inner rhythm is needed so that we know when it is appropriate to speak or to signal the next phase of a meditation. We can only know this intuitively. We have a sense of how the group feels and when the energy is ready to shift into another gear. Many people are anxious that they will get the timing wrong and be insensitive to the group's inner rhythm. The solution to this is not to start off by leading long and complex meditations. Just open and close them, or lead short attunements. It is only practice and experience that brings certainty. You have to learn to trust that what you are feeling in your own body is an accurate sense of the whole group. I still have a tendency to move faster than the inner dynamic of the group, but I can usually feel very clearly in my body when it is time to change focus. Most people feel a certain fragile inner sense of tension which signals the moment to speak and change focus. I also have an inner *Yes/No* flashing light in my head and, when in doubt, I ask *yes?* or *no?* and look to see which light flashes. It sounds simplistic, but it works for me. As the leader I can also choose to exercise leadership and move things along.

Because the meditation leader initiates the tone and rhythm it is important that alongside the sensitivity and rhythm, there is also confidence. This is a very quiet kind of confidence and it comes from being fully present, from being fully in our bodies, grounded and breathing. Even leading a meditation the attitude of Vepassana is appropriate. This is all illusion through which we are breathing. We are learning detachment and compassion.

It is also generally best, in order to avoid inflated egos and for tranquil group harmonics, that people take it in turns to lead meditations.

What to Say?

Some people get carried away leading meditations. I have sat in group meditations with people fuming at the insensitivity, pomposity and stupidity of the leadership. Of course, they ought to have kept on breathing, but sometimes the challenge is too great. I have collapsed in giggles in several meditations. I remember one group which was led like this: *And now that we are calm and relaxed, let us imagine ourselves slipping out of the door and down the stairs. We walk down the street and into the Thomas Cook office where we buy tickets for a wonderful trip. We catch the plane and find ourselves on this wonderful tropical beach lying beside the ocean. A fire is lit for cooking lunch and the vegetarians amongst us now disappear into the jungle to gather fruit and nuts while the rest of us eat the meat and fish...* At that point I had to stifle my giggles and opened my eyes to find several other people, mainly vegetarians, looking around in various states of horror, anger and disbelief.

The funniest story I know is of several Dutch meditation groups which were all being led in the same strange way. This strangeness originated with a woman who had visited the Findhorn Foundation and experienced many group meditations. A phrase much used at the time was *And let us now enter the higher planes,* a reference to higher planes of consciousness. She, however, had heard it as *And let us now enter our aeroplanes.* All across Holland groups were entering aeroplanes to reach higher states of consciousness.

And while in this vein I have my own special plea, which is that I really do not want to hear again *And let us now enter the greater whole...*

If a meditation is being led, it should obviously be for a specific purpose. If there is no specific purpose, then there is no reason to lead it — so let it happen in silence. If there is a clear purpose, then whatever is said has clearly to serve

that purpose and not be superfluous. Group by group, and
situation by situation, we have to be clear about what is
needed. My advice, then, is not to go in to lead a group
meditation without preparation. Unless you are experienced,
do not try to play it by ear. It is helpful to be a bit methodical.
Take a notepad and jot down, first, the purpose of the
meditation. Clear about the purpose, you can then work out
what words will usefully help the group to fulfil that
purpose.

The general map we have been using — that of Center,
Align, Review, Expand, Aware and Serve — can also be
applied to clarifying the purpose and structure of a group
meditation.

Centering and Linking

It may feel appropriate to remind the group to relax. If so,
remember that the key areas to relax are the face muscles
and the solar plexus. You might also remind the group, if it
feels tense, to breathe deeply and draw the air deep into
their diaphragms. With experienced meditators, it is often
unnecessary to lead the centering process.

You may wish to lead the group members into linking
with each other. The techniques and affirmations already
mentioned above can then be used. You might with a small
new group use the *macramé* technique. It cannot though be
used with groups larger than twenty people. For clarity and
as an example that may encourage you to develop your own
method, I will go through it again giving the exact words I
might use:

The group having calmed and relaxed, gently sound out
the first linking:

*Starting on your left and moving in that direction around the
circle, let us link* — pause — *Heart to Heart.*

You will have to be sensitive as to how much time is

required for people to make the links. It should not, however, be longer than about three minutes; it may only take a minute.

Then repeat the same words Starting *on your left and moving in that direction around the circle, let us link* — pause — *Forehead to Forehead.*

Again, wait until the appropriate moment to signal the next stage *Starting on your left and moving in that direction around the circle, let us link* — pause — *Solar Plexus to Solar Plexus.*

Using the macramé technique, I have always found it best to explain to the group in advance what we were going to do.

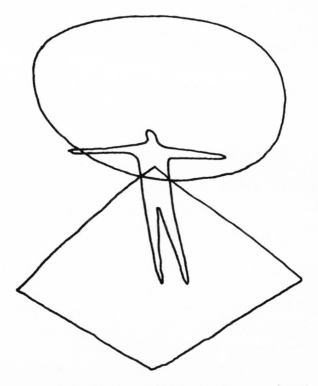

Remembering that we are a link between heaven and earth

With a very large group or with an experienced group, it is usually enough simply to say something like *Let us now link in Love and Peace — Heart to Heart, Mind to Mind, Purpose to Purpose.* Or say simply *We open our hearts to each other.* The group members will then work individually to harmonise with everyone.

Aligning

Quite often, creating these links, relaxing the group and creating a safe atmosphere, will swiftly bring the whole group into alignment. In fact, many people beginning meditation have their very first experience of being aligned with their core self in a group meditation.

If the group needs some extra help to come into alignment, the key technique is to lead the group so that people's hearts are open to each other, but at the same time they need to be clearly focused and linked from the energy space above their heads. The most common form for doing this is to lead the group into placing their focus above their heads. For example, *Let us now become aware of our overlighting group soul/purpose* or *We lift our awareness now into the unity of our core selves.*

Setting the Tone

Often a group only needs a statement that sets the tone of the meditation around which each member can then do their own review, expansion and awareness. In these situations, it is best to wait until the group has begun to settle down and we then gently say the statement or seed thought. The seed thought must, of course, be appropriate and relevant. Whims or inspirations that have recently stimulated us may be of no use at all to the group. It is important to be discriminating and relevant.

Usually it is fairly obvious what is appropriate. Here are

some examples: If the atmosphere has been depressing, for example, then it may be right to drop in a note of joy and understanding—or a note that gives insight or detachment. *As we move into the silence, let us be aware of the qualities of joy and detachment.* If the group has been over-worked or over-excited, then a note of anchoring and comfort may be apt. *Let us be aware of the Earth beneath us and her nurture.*

These group affirmations and notes can be created to suit the occasion, but there is also an enormous fund of religious, mystical and inspirational literature upon which to draw. Sometimes it is appropriate to remind the group of the time of day or the time of year. For example: *We welcome this new day. In a spirit of love let us pass through it recognising the lessons and the unfoldment of each moment.* Or: *As we move towards the Summer Solstice, let us be aware of the intimate relationship between the Earth and the Sun. With gratitude, let us contemplate the mystery of the Sun's relationship with us and with our mother the Earth.*

The statement that sets the tone may, of course, be especially related to that group's current work. If the group is about to embark on a particular project together, it is usually right to sound a note for clarity and cooperation. *As we approach this work, let us do so in a spirit of love and of carefulness.* If there is a tendency towards impatience or irritability, then we might start *In a spirit of patience and tolerance* . . . Or if the group requires inspiring we could start *Remembering that we link heaven and earth...*

Always speak the words slowly, carefully and with due regard to the person in the group with the worst hearing. Gently emphasise and pause on key words; but do not be theatrical. Sincerity without emotionalism is the key to how the voice is best heard leading meditation.

Occasionally, it may seem appropriate to lead the group in a more elaborate way to a particular experience and understanding — for example, to understand the atmosphere of a particular place, or to understand a problem, or to have group consciousness lifted to a particular point of inspiration. This kind of meditation should only be led by someone who has experience and is confident about what they are doing. If you do lead a meditation of this kind, follow the rules of clarity and simplicity. I have heard some meditations which begin with wonderful simplicity and clarity, and then develop into endless rambling novels. Two come to mind immediately. In the first, the leader wanted the group to expand its awareness of the surrounding landscape and plant life. 'As we sit here in the silence, we extend our awareness to the landscape around us. The trees. Hills. Flowers. Shrubs...' And then developed into a horticultural encyclopaedia. The other is a frequent classic in the horror led-meditation stakes. The leader wants us to extend our awareness out from our day-to-day cares to cosmic consciousness. 'We extend our awareness to include the whole planet. The planet becomes a speck and we become aware of our whole solar system...' And so into a postgraduate class in poetic astronomy. Though the worst I ever encountered was a man who wanted us to become more aware of the miracle of our physical bodies. He started by having us enter him on his own breath. 'Now as you enter my lungs you become aware of the rhythm of my breath.' He then took us into his stomach and intestines, and later into most of his organs. This happened incidentally in the same group which had the vegetarians disappearing into the forest.

All this underlines the necessity for a clearly thought-out purpose.

Bring Your Group Back to Earth

At the end of long meditations in which the group has been

led into an expansion of awareness or consciousness, it is usually best to bring the group carefully back and anchor them back into here and now three-dimensional reality. This can be done by reminding the group to be aware of their physical bodies and their breath, to earth themselves again and to be aware of the room in which they are sitting.

Service, Invocation and Radiation

At the end of every group meditation there is an atmosphere of tranquillity and healing and I think that, like individual meditation, it is appropriate for these good vibrations to be radiated outwards. The group leader can say something as simple as *And let us now radiate outwards the healing energy of this meditation — going to where it is needed.* Equally, an invocation or prayer can be used.

Some meditation groups come together for the specific purpose of invoking and radiating healing and love. For many people, this kind of inner work is the most powerful, empowering and satisfying meditation experience. The sensation of flowing and radiating energy is very dynamic and tangible.

The basic principles of group invocation are quite simple. They are virtually the same as those we use when meditating on our own. Essentially, we tune into the need, expand our consciousness to touch realms of love and healing, and then invoke and let the energy flow. In this case we have a definite sequence of activities and it is important that everyone is doing the same thing at the same time. The group, therefore, has to be led to center and alignment, and then through the process of invocation and distribution. The essential sequence is fairly clear:

1. Calm and relax.
2. Cohere as a group. Link in love.
3. Group alignment with group inner self. *We are the*

Workers and the Work. We are One with the One That Is. Or We lift our focus to become aware of our overlighting group soul.

4. With compassion become aware of where healing and love is needed.

5. Lift focus and consciousness up to touch a pure source of Love and Healing.

6. Actively invoke the Love and Healing on behalf of all life.

7. Let it flow.

8. Distribute it. *OM.*

Here is an example of how to lead an invocative meditation taken from my book *Sacred Times*. Done this way it takes about twenty minutes:

Center and align: *Let us sit quietly and each one of us in our own way come to center and alignment.*

Pause.

Linking: *Let us link together in love and in enlightenment as a circle of service.*

Pause.

Group alignment: *We become aware of our overlighting purpose — of the group soul that overlights us.* Pause. *We are the workers and the work. We are one with the one that is.*

Pause.

Awareness of problems: *With the fire of compassion, we become aware of world problems — those areas and situations of conflict, pain, injustice and cruelty and in need of healing.*

Pause — five minutes.

Refocus: *We bring our focus back to this group.* Gentle pause. *And we become aware again of our work and our overlighting purpose.*

Gentle pause.

Focus on Source: *And we become aware, high above us, of a point, a source of love, light and healing. With all our discipline and aspiration, we lift our consciousnesses up to touch that high source of spirit. And with discipline and strength, we hold that high focus.*

Pause — up to five minutes.

Energy flows: *We now sense and recognise the energies of love, light and healing flowing down.* Pause — up to five minutes. *Let the energy come fully down into and through our bodies.*

Gentle pause.

Distribution: *We sense and imagine this energy flowing out to where it is needed.* Pause — up to five minutes. *We release all the energy, holding on to none of it.*

Pause.

Many people feel it appropriate at this point to say an invocative prayer, examples of which are given in the Appendix. Then, if it feels appropriate or you have decided to, sound the OM, either three times or in an open-ended manner. *OM.*

This technique of group invocation always works. Of course, if the members of the group know what they are doing, then no words need in fact be spoken. Or a bell can be used to signal the different phases. If the group has worked together a great deal or if the format is carefully explained beforehand, the bell only needs to be rung four times:

1. Group cohesion and alignment.
2. Compassionate focus on world problems.
3. Peaking and invocation.
4. Distribution.

After the Meditation
Quite often after a group meditation which has focused on invocation, individuals may feel a sense of loss and incompletion. The atmosphere and unity have been so nurturing, comforting and inspiring that to walk away as a

lone individual is a daunting thought. People then may start to grieve the loss of the group, even if they are not conscious of the process. It can be very reassuring to name this process and emotion. In naming it, people get a chance to deal with it. It also provides a trigger to informal discussion after the meditation. Anyone leading a meditation should be sensitive to this sense of loss and allow time for farewells and 'detuning.'

Unless the meditation room is a dedicated sacred area, I usually allow and stimulate conversation after a group meditation. One of the other gifts of conversation is that people are surprised and reassured by how much they have shared a common experience. The group experience of inner realities is not imaginary but tangible. This encourages people in their practice.

If the atmosphere has been particularly high and intense, I usually remind folk to ground themselves and be aware of the three-dimensional world. If the atmosphere has been particularly poignant and sensitive, I usually point out that they might now be unusually emotionally vulnerable and that they might want to be aware of this and close down their energies. This is done simply by focusing back inside our own physical bodies, making sure our heads and torsos are grounded, and re-adopting a realistic attitude. People can also be reminded that if they meditate on their own later that day they can contemplate the experience of the group meditation and see what it teaches them as they sit on their own.

Sometimes it is also pleasant and reassuring to bless the group, but as always keep it simple and sincere. *May the blessings of Gaia and All That Is be with each of us as we travel home. Blessed be.* Be careful, though, not to use words that sound pompous, twee or belong to a specific religion, thereby offending others of another faith.

The Planetary Network of Light

A few words on the planetary network of light: This phrase refers to the conscious telepathic and intuitive linking of meditators across the planet. Many thousands of people are consciously working at creating these links. The underlying idea is that if we all link up and focus, on a daily basis, on radiating tranquillity and enlightenment together, we can affect the atmosphere of the whole planet. From your private experience in meditation, this will either be believable to you or not.

Most of us who meditate, however, have come to an intuitive and experiential understanding that energy indeed follows thought. The creation of a meditational planetary network of light is, therefore, a very real and powerful idea. It is a way in which all of us, regardless of our social or work situation, can work together to change the atmosphere of humanity's contemporary culture. Our culture is too harsh, too savage, too materialistic, too insensitive. Energy follows thought and we can meditate together to radiate and create a new culture. This perhaps may seem fantastic, but it follows the natural logic of the whole meditation experience. If it seems appropriate to you then, you may want consciously to link up with other meditation groups and with other meditating individuals across the planet. Some of them you may know only by name and reputation. Others you may know personally. You may also, for instance, tune into the planetary network of churches, temples, mosques, synagogues and other places of worship. You may also link in with particular communities or particular places on the Earth. Some people work in specific meditation triangles forming a link with two other individuals.

Even if we do not consciously create or work with these links, I believe that it is happening anyway at a subconscious telepathic level. We are energetically connected cells in the total body of humanity and the planet. My understanding is that the reclusive meditator is not engaged in a narcissistic relationship that evades the real world, but that the process of individual meditation is part of the transformation of all life.

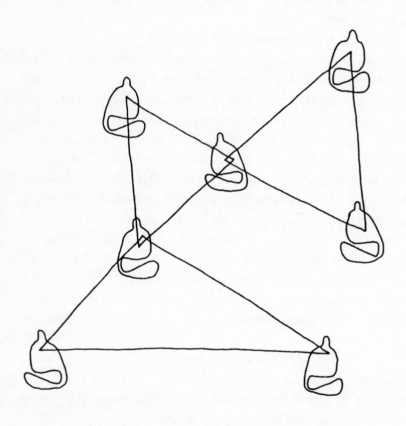

Creating the planetary network of light

Appendix

In this Appendix there are various pieces of extra information which I hope readers will find useful or stimulating.

Practical Hints on Relaxation and Stress Control

Because so many people begin to meditate as a way of achieving relaxation and of controlling stress in their everyday lives, it seems useful to give some extra advice on this subject. Over time, of course, the benefits of daily meditation anyway spill over into a more relaxed and integrated attitude to life. There are, however, certain attitudes and techniques which may be immediately useful. None of this is to deny, however, that we might need in fact to look at the whole way in which we lead our lives. No amount of relaxation or meditation will work on a dedicated speedfreak. Working, for instance, in an electronic amusement arcade may also not be helpful. First, there are a few helpful keywords:

1. Intention.
2. Breathing.
3. Body Language.
4. Detachment.
5. Understanding.

Intention

We cannot achieve relaxation unless we have a clear and committed intention. To become relaxed, to control stress, requires clear resolve. It requires a clear inner decisiveness — for, of course, nobody except each individual has control over their life. We, therefore, need to make certain that we have the right attitude. We need to be certain that we really mean to change and we have to be prepared to work to achieve what we want.

We need, therefore, to make the commitment. We need to state clearly to ourself in meditation, 'I am committed to becoming relaxed and calm. This is my clear decision.'

Within meditation, during the period of review, we can then begin to use an exercise in which we imagine ourselves in those situations which cause stress. We imagine ourselves in these situations — and then we experience and imagine ourselves being totally calm and relaxed in them. Build up a self-image of yourself as un-stressed and in control.

Breathing

Whenever you feel stress, breathe calmly.

When you feel stress, focus on your breath and let it come down deep into your lungs. Feel the tension that exists in the lower part of your diaphragm. Calm your breathing and bring it deep into yourself. Do it gently, but with self-discipline.

If you are in a situation where it is possible — for example travelling — begin to count your breaths to a hundred. Demonstrate to yourself that you are in control of your breathing and of your body. You are relaxed and in control.

Body Language

Be careful about your body language in situations of stress. Relax your shoulders, your neck and your face muscles. Gently relax your solar plexus.

Then make certain that you look calm and serene.

Even if you want to behave completely hysterically, make sure your appearance is relaxed and dignified. Imagine that your body is really elegant, relaxed and content. The calm of your body language will overspill into your psychological attitude. You are in calm control.

Detachment

Well, really! What are you doing taking it all so seriously? You are a fine and wonderful human being even if no one in this situation recognises it. Be detached about it. Have a sense of perspective. Don't be a slave. Don't take it all so seriously.

Deliberately, work on this attitude in your meditations.

Understanding

We can use meditation to come to an understanding of why we feel stress.

In meditation, calm and aligned, we can begin to examine what it is that puts pressure on us. What are its sources? What is its history? Why are we so vulnerable? Which part of our ego is involved?

We can examine whether the major anxiety lies in our body, emotions, mind or our general personality. We can learn about ourselves in the calm and the empathy of meditation. If we understand ourselves, we can liberate ourselves from anxiety.

Mantrams, Prayers and Affirmations

There are many very beautiful and inspiring mantrams, prayers and affirmations. Here are a few that particularly touch me or which I find particularly useful for different situations and moods.

"I am a Being far greater and grander than I have as yet conceived. I am unfolding gradually but surely into higher planes of consciousness. I am moving Forward and Upward constantly. My goal is the Realisation of the True Self, and I welcome each stage of Unfoldment that leads me towards my aim. I am a manifestation of reality. I *AM*."

(Yogi Ramacharaka, *Raja Yoga*)

Here and Now

Let Light beyond flame Light within.
Enlightenment

Let Love beyond flame Love within.
Illumination.

Let Power beyond flame Power within.
Emancipation.

Life beyond flames Life within.

Enlightenment. Illumination. Emancipation.

Bless the World

Love to All Beings
North — South — East — West
Above — Below
Love to All Beings

Compassion to All Beings
North — South — East — West
Above — Below
Compassion to All Beings
Joy to All Beings
North — South — East — West
Above — Below
Joy to All Beings

Peace to All Beings
North — South — East — West
Above — Below
Peace to All Beings

The Gayatri

O Thou Who givest sustenance to the universe,
From whom all things proceed
To whom all things return,
Unveil to us the face of the true Spiritual Sun
Hidden by a disc of golden Light
That we may know the Truth
And do our whole duty
As we journey to Thy sacred feet.

A Glastonbury Invocation

There is a Source of Love which is
The Heart of All Life.
Let that Love flow
Source to Earth
Heart to Heart.

There is a Source of Light which is
the Mind of All Life.
Let that Light flow
Source to Earth
Mind to Mind.

There is a Source of Power which is
the Purpose of All Life.
Let that Power flow
Source to Earth
Purpose to Purpose.

We are that Light
We are that Love
We are that Power.

Peace and Healing on Earth.

More radiant than the Sun,
Purer than the snow.
Subtler than the ether,
Is the Self,
The spirit within my heart.
I am that Self,
That self am I.

I am one with my group brothers and sisters
And all that I have is theirs.
May the love which is in my soul pour forth to them.
May the strength which is in me lift and aid them.
May the thoughts which my soul creates, reach
and encourage them.

We are the workers — and the Work.
We are one — with the One That Is.

The Mantram of Unification

The children of humanity are one and I am one with them.
I seek to love, not hate;
I seek to serve and not exact due service;
I seek to heal, not hurt.

Let pain bring due reward of light and love.
Let the soul control the outer form,
And life, and all events,
And bring to light the Love
That underlies the happenings of the time.

Let vision come and insight.
Let the future stand revealed.
Let inner union demonstrate and outer cleavages be gone.
Let love prevail.
Let all humanity love.

May the Sun in the head
And the Sun in the heart
Respond to the life emanating
From the Central Spiritual Sun
That the service of love
May be rendered with perfection.

Kwan Yin Pledge

Never will I seek nor receive private, individual salvation.
Never will I enter into final peace alone.
But forever, and everywhere, will I live and strive for the redemption of every creature throughout the world.

OM MANI PADME HUM

This Sanskrit phrase means, "Oh, the Jewel in the Lotus."
Or, "Oh, my God within Me."

For City Dwellers

Cactus rose in the desert.
Seaweed on the ocean.
Pine tree in the mountains.
Buttercup in the meadow.
Rich Earth beneath.
Spiritual Sun around.

Everything breathes.

O Hidden Life vibrant in every atom,
O Hidden Light shining in every creature,
O Hidden Love embracing all in Oneness,
May each one who feels herself as One with Thee,
Know She is therefore One with every other.

(Annie Besant)

The Great Invocation

From the Point of Light within the Mind of God
Let Light stream forth into the minds of men.
Let Light descend on Earth.

From the Point of Love within the Heart of God
Let Love stream forth into the hearts of men.
May Christ return to Earth.

From the Centre where the Will of God is known,
Let Purpose guide the little wills of men,
The Purpose which the Masters know and serve.

From the centre which we call the race of men
Let the Plan of Love and Light work out
And may it seal the door where evil dwells.

Let Light and Love and Power
Restore the Plan on Earth.

The Lord's Prayer

Our Father which art in Heaven, Hallowed be Thy Name.
Thy kingdom come. Thy will be done on Earth as it is in
Heaven. Give us this day our daily bread and forgive us
our trespasses as we forgive them that trespass against us.
And lead us not into temptation but deliver us from evil
— for Thine is the Kingdom, the Power and the Glory. For
ever and ever. Amen.

To the Elements

Creature of fire let me unite with you that I may have
   passion and power.
Creature of water let me unite with you that I may have
   fluid movement.
Creature of air let me unite with you that I may have
   wisdom and intuition.
Creature of earth let me unite with you that I may have
   stability and steadfastness.

                                          (Diane Mariechild)

Blessed be thou Creatress of Life whose love forever shines
within me. Help me to use thy energy to direct my force.
Light my path that I may follow it in love, secure in the
knowledge that I move from a source deep within me. Let
me use my energy to create the world anew. Instill in me an
awareness of the rhythms and cycles of nature so that I may
intuitively know the time to build up and the time to tear
down; the time to speak and the time to remain silent; the
time to move and the time to be still. Let me sense now and
always the depth of our connections. For we are all one
and the force that holds us together is love.

Salutation of Life

I AM but One among the Many.
I AM but One among the Few.
I AM all that One, within the ALL.
I AM the future within all time.
I exist in Reality and in the infinite
The World and I are One.
All that is Life, revolves within me.
Now I am a Unit of Being, and do therefore
claim mine own identity within a
World of life.

I AM

(Hermes Trismegistus, *Thirteenth Emerald Tablet*)

There is but One Life — One Life Underlying. This Life is
manifesting through ME, and through every other shape,
form and thing. I am resting on the bosom of the Great
Ocean of Life, and it is supporting me, and will carry me
safely, though the waves rise and fall — though the storms
rage and the tempests roar. I am safe on the Ocean of Life,
and rejoice as I feel the sway of its motion. Nothing can
harm me — though changes may come and go, I am Safe. I
am One with the All Life, and its Power. Knowledge and
Peace are behind, underneath and within Me. O! One Life!
Express Thyself through me — carry me now on the crest of
the wave, now deep down in the trough of the ocean —
supported always by Thee — all is good to me, as I feel Thy
life moving in and through me. I am Alive, through Thy life,
and I open myself to Thy full manifestation and inflow.
(Yogi Ramachraka, *Raja Yoga*)

The Mantram of Service

May the Power of the One Life
pour through the group of all true servers.

May the Love of the One Soul
characterise the lives of all who seek to aid the Greater
Purpose.

May we fulfil our part in the One Work
through self-forgetfulness, harmlessness and right speech.

I am a messenger of Light. I am a pilgrim on the way of Love.
I do not walk alone but know myself as one with all great
souls — and one with them in service.
Their strength is mine. This strength I claim.
My strength is theirs — and this I freely give.
As a soul, I walk on Earth.
I represent the One.

Here I am, God.
Use me in any way.

Into your hands Beloved Spirit, I place my whole being —
my heart, my mind, my soul, my strength, my spirit. I ask
you to use me. Use me as you will to bring about your
wonders and glories so all humanity may come to know
you, to love you and to put you first in everything. Thank
you Beloved Spirit that this is so. So be it.

For Expectant Mothers

Mother of all life,
Ocean of creation,
Draw me into the deep waves of your embrace.

Nurturing within,
Silent without,
Never seeking,
Ever peace.

You are my centre.
My circle, infinite horizon.
Life within.
Life beyond.
Growth is the power of love.

I
am
Silent growth in power.

The Prayer to Shambhala

Thou Who called me to the path of labour,
accept my ableness and my desire.
Accept my labour, O Lord, because by day
and by night Thou beholdest me.
Manifest thy hand, O Lord, because
great is the darkness. I follow Thee!

Prayer of Yellow Lark, Sioux Indian Chief

O Great Spirit, whose voice I hear in the wind, and whose breath gives life to all the world, hear me. I come before You, one of Your many children. I am small and weak. I need Your strength and wisdom. Let me walk in beauty, and make my eyes behold the red and purple sunset. Make my hands respect the things You have made, my ears sharp to hear Your voice. Make me wise, so that I may know the things You have taught my people, the lessons You have hidden in every leaf and rock. I seek strength not to be superior to my sisters and brothers, but to be able to fight my greatest enemy — myself. Make me ever ready to come to You with clean hands and straight eyes, so when Life fades as a fading sunset, my spirit may come to you without shame.

Sense the protection of the parents - Earth and Cosmos

I am no longer dark and alone
as I bathe in the light of my source

The Great Tree of Peace of the Iroquois

The Tree of the Great Peace has been planted:
Hear me, brothers and sisters, friends and relatives;
It is true the Great Tree of Peace has been planted,
And the Great White Roots of Peace have spread out
To embrace and hold us all.
Yes, it is true that we all are related.
Let the eyes of your eyes see,
Let the ears of your ears hear,
The spark of the universe —
It is the oneness of life.
And with hands reaching out
Trace the roots to their source, and
Be welcome beneath the Great Tree of Peace.
Onen

                              (Wayne Eagleboy)

Song of the Sky Loom

Oh our Mother the Earth, oh our Father the Sky,
Your children are we, and with tired backs
We bring you the gifts that you love.
Then weave for us a garment of brightness:
May the warp be the white light of morning,
May the weft be the red light of evening,
May the fringes be the falling rain,
May the border be the standing rainbow.
Thus weave for us a garment of brightness

Divine Mother, open wide the bud of my devotion and release its fragrance, that it may spread from my soul to the souls of all others, ever whispering of Thee.

I will light the match of smiles. My gloom veil will disappear. I shall behold my soul in the light of my smiles, hidden behind the accumulated darkness of ages. When I find myself, I shall race through all hearts with the torch of my soul-smiles. My heart will smile first, then my eyes and my face. Every body-part will shine in the light of smiles.

I will run amid the thickets of melancholy hearts and make a bonfire of all sorrows. I am the irresistible fire of smiles. I will fan myself with the breeze of God-joy and blaze my way through the darkness of all minds. My smiles will convey the smiles of God and whoever meets me will catch a whiff of my divine joy. I will carry fragrant purifying torches of smiles for all hearts.

(Paramahansa Yogananda, *Metaphysical Meditations*)

That we may walk fittingly where grass is green,
Oh our Mother the Earth, Oh our Father the Sky!

(From *Songs of the Tewa*)

An Ending and Blessing

There is a peace that passes all understanding; it abides in the hearts of those who live in the eternal. There is a power that makes all things new; it lives and moves in those who know the self as one.

May that peace brood over us, that power uplift us, until we stand where the One Initiator is invoked, until we see the Star of Initiation shine forth.

(Adapted from the Liberal Catholic Liturgy)

Meditation of the Dove

This is an extremely easy and very beautiful structured meditation which can be used by individuals or groups. It brings an experience of pure love and healing. I am putting it into this book as an example of quite a complex meditation which yields a very interesting atmosphere and dynamic:

(a) Sitting quietly and centered, imagine a circle of *twelve* points around you at waist height.
(b) Then imagine another circle of *seven* points around you at heart level.
(c) Imagine a further circle of *three* points around your head.
(d) And then a *single* point above you.
(e) Then high above, sense a great white Dove; from its breast pours a pure blessing of love, grace and healing.
(f) Let the love and healing flow down through you and out to where it is needed.

This meditation can last either five or twenty-five minutes. It can be done simply — just counting off the points in each tier, e.g. *One, two, three* ... Or it can be done with more care, for instance by lighting a candle for each point or by specifically naming them. On the next page is a suggested format for conducting this meditation in a more elaborate way. If it is done by a group, a glass of water can be shared at the end as a form of communion.

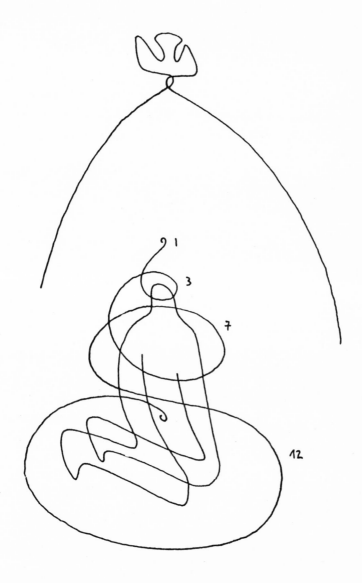

The wedding cake of energy circles - 12, 7, 3, 1 - for the Dove Meditation

More Detailed Format for Dove Meditation

1. Relax. Become calm. Link in Love with those who are in your meditation group.

2. Focus quietly in your mind's eye and be spiritually aware and awake.

3. In a natural and calm rhythm, name or sense the first level of twelve points clockwise around you: *Aries — Taurus — Gemini — Cancer — Leo — Virgo — Libra — Scorpio — Sagittarius — Capricorn — Aquarius — Pisces.*
Pause.

4. In calm rhythm, name and sense the second level of seven points around you: *Rhythm — Devotion — Structure — Harmony — Enlightenment — Illumination — Power.*
Pause.

5. In calm rhythm, name and sense the third higher level of three points: *Light — Love — Spirit.*
Pause.

6. Sense and name the single highest point above them all: *Infinity.*
Pause.

7. Know and sense that there is a great Dove on high. Be aware of its sacramental energy of Peace and Healing pouring down through you and the group.
Pause.

8. Sense the Healing and Peace flowing out to where it is needed.

9. You may if you wish sound out three times OM in order to ensure the distribution of the energy.

10. If you wish you may share a glass of water that has been in the center of the group from the beginning.

Revision Notes

A while ago, Corinne McLaughlin of the Sirius Community in Massachussets produced a two-page sheet entitled *Notes on Meditation*. It is concise and extremely useful. It is included in this Appendix for two reasons. First, readers may be interested in reading how another teacher of meditation approaches the subject. Second, you may want to use it as a memory aid.

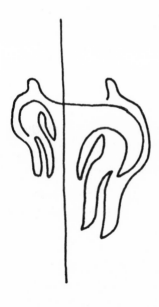

1. Create a regular time each day and a regular place for your meditation.

2. Begin by sitting comfortably, spine erect, body relaxed yet alert.

3. Focus on your breath; slow deep rhythmic breathing calms the body.

4. Still your emotions, observing them without identifying with them. Visualize your feelings as a clear, still lake, reflecting the higher consciousness of the soul/inner self.

5. Methods for stilling the mind:

   (a) Become a detached observer of your thoughts, watching them go by without seeking to force them to stop (like watching birds flying past); say to yourself: *I have a mind, but I am not my mind.* Disidentify from your mind and simply witness it.

   (b) Listen to the inner sound inside your head and keep your awareness solely on it.

   (c) Repeat an inspirational word or phrase over and over to yourself, eg: *OM — Love — I am the Soul — Be still and know that I am God/Goddess/name of a saint* .

   (d) Visualize an image of light, love or beauty in the center of your forehead, e.g. a sun, heart, flower, diamond, star.

6. Intention of meditation should be to contact the soul, one's inner divinity, for inspiration, rather than become passive.

7. Types of meditation:

   (a) *Reflective meditation*: Reflect on an inspirational seed thought or a short passage. Think about its various meanings, aspects, applications to your life. Focus on the positive aspects only. (e.g. *Be joyful, for joy lets in the Light; Humanity is holy; All is unity; I seek to love, not hate; Be here now.*)

(b) *Receptive Meditation*: Lift your consciousness through aspiration, dedication and will to soul awareness, identifying with the greater Whole, oneness with all life, our universal aspect — the God presence within us. Open up, become receptive, yet alert. Avoid negative passivity and drowsiness. Keep an attitude of waiting and inner silence.

Experiences in receptive meditation might include any of the following:

- Seeing images or visions or illumination, the revelation of the Divinity immanent in all things.
- Direct knowing, or intuition about the true nature, essence or purpose of something; a deeper or broader understanding.
- Inner contact or alignment with the soul, or God presence — to harmonise, energise and inspire.
- Hearing a message of an impersonal character relating to your spiritual growth. These are usually short, direct, meaningful and inspirational if coming from the highest source within you. (If messages are overly dramatic, glamorous and ego-inflating they are probably coming from your subconscious desires or from the astral/psychic level and should be ignored. Discriminate.)
- Inner dialogue with your higher self or soul, the wise being within you.
- An experience of energy, vibration or colour that brings a feeling of expansion, or centeredness or peacefulness.
- An urge to action as service for the good of humanity.

- Delayed reception of impression; inspiration or intuition coming later when needed or seemingly as confirmation from an outside source.

(c) *Creative meditation*: Use your mind creatively to build positive thoughts about yourself, about other people, about the world, and to overcome negative emotions, bad health etc. Energise your thoughts.

8. End your meditation with a blessing: Radiate outwards the energy built up during the meditation by visualising light and love flowing out to humanity and to all life. As we give, so also we receive.

Meditation 'Clinic' Hints

At my own Meditation 'Clinics' I also give out a short memory aid which readers may also find helpful:

1. Grounding and being present.

Meditation is about being present — not daydreaming or being 'out there.' So you have to be fully in your body. The best technique is to ensure that you are grounded and earthed. Feel and sense your body energies and consciousness rooted in the earth. Your spine as the trunk of a tree with roots. Energy coming out of the base of your spine and feet, and going deep into the earth.

95% of folk who fall asleep in meditation are not grounded.

2. Body language.

Spine straight = alert consciousness.

Serene facial expression = present and in control.

3. Breath.

Whatever else is going on: physical tension and pain; emotional irritation and uncontrollable feelings; manic wandering mind — KEEP BREATHING. The breath must always be smooth and regular. You breathe through your tensions. You bring yourself present to your tensions, observer to them. When all is well, you don't have to think about your breath at all.

Two basic breaths:

(a) The in-breath and out-breath flow smoothly in and out of each other; no break in between. Smooth in-out-in-out-in . . . Placed anywhere in the chest, high, middle, low or through all of it.

(b) Count to 7 on in breath. Pause for 1. Count to 7 on out-breath. Pause for 1. Etc. So it is 7-1-7-1.

If your chest is tight and breath is shallow, the quickest release is to exhale as far as you can, pushing the air out and then out even more until it hurts. The in-rush of air is then wonderful.

4. Relaxation.
Allow relaxation into you. Be patient about it.

5. Distractions.
Never judge what is happening when you sit. Just observe yourself — but keep breathing. You only need to bring your focus back to breathing when you become distracted by your body, feelings or mind.

6. More distraction?
It is normal and healthy to spend a while, perhaps the first 5-15 minutes letting your mind contemplate your life and what's at the top of your consciousness. I call this 'clearing the desk.'

7. Crazy mind?
Well, focus it on something that interests you. Contemplate God or your chakras or Gaia... See what your consciousness picks up.

The Lunar Cycle and Solar Festivals[1]

I like to encourage people to explore in meditation the Full Moon rhythm, the Solstices, Equinoxes and the Fire Festivals. I am enthusiastic about this because these moments are power points in time and are part of the natural ecological rhythm of our planetary environment. In the days before organised religions, these natural signals stimulated individual and communal spiritual activity. In a time when we are discarding the unnecessary restraints of religious dogma and when we are regaining a true awareness of earth and our environment, I find it very useful to allow my awareness to be touched by these significant times. I also very much like the fact that even if there were no people at all on the earth, these pulsations in activity would nevertheless be there. To work with them, therefore, is to increase our attunement to our environment.

The Lunar Cycle

Many people find it useful to let the rhythm of the lunar cycle influence their meditation. This may on first hearing sound spooky, but there are grounded reasons for this.

The full moons are helpful for several reasons:

1. In the same way that the moon magnetically pulls the Earth's oceans, so she also magnetically aids human spiritual work by increasing the vibratory rate of our bodies; this means that at the time of the full moons we can be more sensitive and aware.

2. The lunar cycle can be seen wherever we are upon the planet and can therefore be used as a planetwide signal for

[1] The information in this section is also on the educational poster *Celebrate The Year — The Annual Cycle of Spiritual Festivals* and is expanded on in my book *Sacred Times — A New Approach to Festivals* both of which are available from the Findhorn Press.

networking the widest possible group meditation and invocation.

3. Due to the fact that throughout human history, the full moons have been used as a signal for spiritual festivals, there is a powerful inner energy pattern already associated with the full moons. By following this archetypal inner pattern, our own spiritual work is made easier.

4. In the same way that the moon creates the oceans' tides and affects physical and growth rhythms in the plant, animal and human realms, so it is appropriate that we should flow with this same rhythm in our inner and spiritual work. It puts us in ecological attunement with our greater environment.

In the most general way: When the moon is dark, it is appropriate to be more reflective and contemplative. At the time of the new moon one's meditation becomes more active, building up to a peak of creative inner work at the time of the full moon. So the basic rhythm is:

Dark/No Moon = Reflection, Contemplation

New Moon = More active inner work

Full Moon = Peak of creative inner work

The full moon is a time for active inner growth and service. It is a time to reach for the very highest. Each full moon is a global signal for invoking, channelling and distributing love and healing. The full moon is also a signal for climaxing personal change.

The Five Days around Each Full Moon

Many people find it helpful to keep to a certain format for the five days around the full moon.

1. For the two days preceding the full moon, your major focus can be upon becoming aware of the needs of your environment and of the planet. You tune into the needs of

the planet and begin to reach up to invoke and channel the needed energies.

2. The actual day of the moon is one of intense invocation.

3. The two days following the moon are then oriented to distributing the energy.

The new moon can be used as a signal to orient yourself to this work. Many people, for the five days of the full moon, make a point of meditating at dawn, at noon, at five o'clock and at dusk. You, can if you want, imagine yourself networking with all these other meditators.

The Annual Rhythm of the Full Moons — Easter, Wesak and World Invocation Day

Many meditators keep to an annual rhythm which builds up to a particularly intense period of spiritual work around the times of the full moons of Aries, Taurus and Gemini in April, May and June.

The peak of this intense spiritual work is thought to occur at the time of the Taurus full moon, a festival which is known as Wesak. Wesak is known in the East as the time of the Buddha's birthday and there is a legend which tells that at Wesak the Buddha, the Christ and all the other exceptional beings of our planet come together in the same geographical location in order to perform together a great spiritual invocation — the climax of the annual rhythm of spiritual service.

The rhythm of these three full moons of April, May and June is similar to the rhythm of the five days around each full moon.

The Aries full moon holds a general note of tuning into the planet's problems and of compassion, and is also known, of course, as the Easter or Christ Festival

The Wesak full moon has an intense focus on reaching to

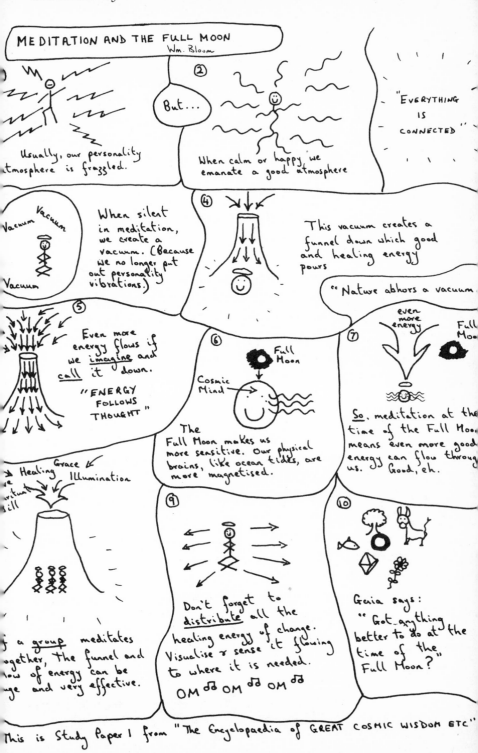

MEDITATION AND THE FULL MOON
Wm. Bloom

Usually, our personality atmosphere is frazzled.

② But...

When calm or happy, we emanate a good atmosphere

"EVERYTHING IS CONNECTED"

Vacuum Vacuum Vacuum Vacuum — When silent in meditation, we create a vacuum. (Because we no longer put out personality vibrations.)

④ This vacuum creates a funnel down which good and healing energy pours

"Nature abhors a vacuum"

⑤ Even more energy flows if we imagine and call it down. "ENERGY FOLLOWS THOUGHT"

⑥ Cosmic Mind Full Moon The Full Moon makes us more sensitive. Our physical brains, like ocean tides, are more magnetised.

⑦ even more energy Full Moon So, meditation at the time of the Full Moon means even more good energy can flow through us. Good, eh.

Healing Grace Illumination — ... a group meditates together, the funnel and flow of energy can be huge and very effective.

⑨ Don't forget to distribute all the healing energy of change. Visualise & sense it flowing to where it is needed. OM ♩♩ OM ♩♩ OM ♩♩

⑩ Gaia says: "Got anything better to do at the time of the Full Moon?"

This is Study Paper 1 from "The Encyclopaedia of GREAT COSMIC WISDOM ETC" touch the very highest help that is available and creating a channel for it.

The Gemini full moon has a general orientation of invocation and, most importantly, distribution to ensure that all the energy that has been brought down in the preceding two months is sent out to where it is needed. The Gemini full moon is called by some people World Invocation Day.

The Lunar Cycle and Personal Growth

The lunar cycle can be used not only for planetary service, but also to help one pass through difficult personality changes, through expansions of consciousness and through surrenderings to new psychological patterns. The keys to using the full moon rhythms in this way are *self-discipline* and a *will-to-change*.

The method of using the lunar cycle is as follows:

1. For a period of time leading up to the full moon, meditate upon and contemplate the change you wish to make. The dark side of the moon can be used for deep and honest inner contemplation of oneself. At the time of the new moon, begin to orient yourself fully to the change or awareness that is to be achieved. The new moon marks a time of *positive* contemplation and clear intention.

2. Some days before the full moon, by an act of will make the change, reach for the new awareness — and then hold it. Experience it fully in meditation. This requires careful self-discipline.

3. Hold the change or new awareness until the actual time of the full moon.

4. After the full moon, *relax* completely, release all tension and striving, release even the aspiration to change — be patient now, kind to yourself and assess the change.

5. It is very important that all the way through the

exercise you remain fully aware of and involved in the work of invocation. This energy of invocation and the aspiration to serve through meditation profoundly aids one's own growth patterns.

This whole rhythm and exercise can, of course, always be repeated.

This use of the full moons for personal growth can also be applied to the annual cycle, using Wesak and the Aries and Gemini full moons. It can be used for substantial and very difficult changes. The method, then, is the same as above except that the time scale of the exercise is longer. We start contemplating our change several months before Wesak. We then build up focus and self-discipline actually to make the change several weeks before Wesak, preferably at the Aries full moon. The change and point of tension is then held up to Wesak and then gradually relaxed over the Gemini full moon. The effects of this technique can be quite transformatory.

The Quality of Each Full Moon

Each full moon also has a distinctive quality and atmosphere which is associated with the Sun sign in which it appears. Careful attunement at each full moon can bring very helpful and deep insights into the sun sign in which it appears and into the lessons of that particular zodiacal constellation. The Tibetan teacher, Djwahl Kuhl, translated into English ancient keynotes for each sign of the Zodiac which can be used as seed-thoughts. These keynotes are particularly relevant to stages in human spiritual growth. They can also be incorporated into group full moon meditations.

Aries: I come forth and from the plane of mind I rule.
Taurus: I see and when the eye is opened, all is light.
Gemini: I recognise my other self and in the waning of that self, I grow and glow.

Cancer: I build a lighted house and therein dwell.
Leo: I am That and That am I.
Virgo: I am the mother and the child. I, God, I, matter, am.
Libra: I choose the way which leads between the two great lines of force.
Scorpio: Warrior I am and from the battle I emerge triumphant.
Sagittarius: I see the goal. I reach that goal and then I see another.
Capricorn: Lost am I in light supernal, yet on that light I turn my back.
Aquarius: Water of life am I, poured forth for thirsty men.
Pisces: I leave the Father's home and turning back, I save.

Full Moon Dates 1996–2003
The following dates are correct for Greenwich Mean Time but may vary by one day according to your time zone.

1996		*1997*		*1998*	
Jan	5	Jan	23	Jan	12
Feb	4	Feb	22	Feb	11
March	5	March	24	March	13
April	4	April	22	April	11
May	3	May	22	May	11
June	1	June	20	June	10
July	1	July	20	July	9
July	30	August	18	August	8
August	28	Sep	16	Sep	6
Sep	27	Oct	16	Oct	5
Oct	26	Nov	14	Nov	4
Nov	25	Dec	14	Dec	3
Dec	24				

1999

Jan	2
Jan	31
March	2
March	31
April	30
May	30
June	28
July	28
August	26
Sep	25
Oct	24
Nov	23
Dec	22

2000

Jan	21
Feb	19
March	20
April	18
May	18
June	16
July	16
August	15
Sep	13
Oct	13
Nov	11
Dec	11

2001

Jan	9
Feb	8
March	9
April	8
May	7
June	6
July	5
Aug	4
Sep	2
Oct	2
Nov	1
Nov	30
Dec	30

2002

Jan	28
Feb	27
March	28
April	27
May	26
June	24
July	24
Aug	22
Sep	21
Oct	21
Nov	20
Dec	19

2003

Jan	18
Feb	16
March	18
April	16
May	16
June	14
July	13
Aug	12
Sep	10
Oct	10
Nov	9
Dec	8

The Solar and Fire Festivals

It is extremely interesting to follow in meditation the great ancient festivals of the Sun.

The Solstices are the major solar events. They occur at the times of the longest day and the shortest day in the year. June 21/2 and December 21/22. They celebrate and acknowledge the crucial relationship that exists between all life on Earth and the Sun.

Life on Earth is totally dependent upon the energy of the Sun. Without the Sun's warmth and light, there would be no life as we know it. We live not on an isolated planet, but on a planet which is an orbiting part of the Sun's solar system. The Sun nurtures Earth and is, so to speak, the Earth's older spiritual sister. The bond between Earth and Sun is intimate and the relationship is delicate. The Earth shares the same energy field of the Sun and, in a very real sense, draws its life force from her. The Earth's prana or life-force is that of the Sun.

The Solstices are celebrated for several different reasons:

1. In gratitude to the Sun, acknowledging our ecological dependence.

2. Simply to celebrate the passage of time.

3. In a more esoteric way, spiritual ceremony and ritual help build an energy temple that aids and enhances the flow of the Sun's energy across Earth. Ancient religions used harmonically constructed temples and careful ritual to help this ecological relationship between fertility and the Sun.

4. And philosophically, the relationship of the Sun with Earth can also be interpreted as symbolic of certain great spiritual truths. These truths, which are concerned with the very nature of human and cosmic incarnation, are told through the various fables of the sacrifice of a Sun deity who later resurrects.

The Winter Solstice
The Winter Solstice is the shortest day of the year and occurs on December 21st. It marks the time of the greatest darkness, but also the beginning of all that is new, bringing light, warmth and vitality. That which is planted may now begin to grow. It is a time of hope for it promises the renewal and rebirth of all things. In the West it is celebrated as the time of the birth of the Christ incarnation in Jesus. This is also the day when the child Horus of the Egyptian Mysteries is reborn and also Iacchus-Dionysus of the Orphic Mysteries.

The Summer Solstice
The Summer solstice marks the longest day of the year and occurs on June 21st. It is the day of the greatest outpouring of solar energy and is sometimes known as the Festival of Joy. Whilst priests and priestesses may celebrate the event in profound ceremonies, other folk enjoy a time of festive communal gathering, dancing and other enjoyable forms of communication. The height of the Summer light is known, but now come the shorter days and longer nights — so within it all, there is also a note of poignancy and an understanding of the deeper rhythms of life.

Northern and Southern Hemispheres
Of course, while those north of the Equator celebrate the Summer Solstice, those south of the Equator celebrate the Winter Solstice. This holds an interesting insight into the nature of Earth. Her nature is always in a state of flux. While darkness covers one side, the other side is in light. While one hemisphere celebrates the longest day, the other celebrates the shortest. The famous Ying-Yang symbol of the circle divided into a black side and white side demonstrates this same nature; the line dividing the two is not straight, but undulates.

The Spring and Autumn Equinoxes

The Equinoxes mark the time when the Sun's annual pathway and the celestial equator intersect. This occurs twice in the year, at the Spring Equinox on March 21st and at the Autumn Equinox on September 21st. These two dates also mark the half-way points between the Summer and Winter Solstices. They were important to the ancients simply because of their marking of the passage of time. They have greater importance, however, in connection with the planting and harvesting of crops. Of course, the two dates do not coincide exactly with when crops are, in fact, planted and harvested, for these times vary according to geography. The festivals associated with the two Equinoxes are, therefore, moveable and coincide with the local rhythms of growth of the plant kingdom. Crucially, then, the Equinox festivals are concerned not only with the passage of the Sun, but also with invoking the help of the forces of nature.

The Spring Equinox

As Spring approaches, the forces of nature — sometimes recognised as nature elementals and angels of the harvest — who have been in a form of meditative contemplation through the cold of Winter, begin gently to reawaken. The seeds and bulbs in the earth, the roots and the new branches-to-be of the trees, are calling to them.

In our Spring festivals we recognise the nature forces and their work. We address them with offerings of respect, of cooperation and of joy — with gifts, with dance, with ritual, with play, with meditation and with worship. We also recognise the fertility and nature of our Earth Mother, the Goddess.

The Autumn Equinox

By the Autumn Equinox the major work of nature's invisible helpers has been completed. Their annual rhythm of holding the vision of how the plant kingdom should grow and blossom, and their careful tending of that plan, has ended. It has been intense but beautiful work and now they are ready to retire and enter again into that contemplative meditation in preparation for next year's growth. Before they retire, however, they dance in great fairy and angel rings affirming their community until they work together again in the following Spring.

In the harvest festivals and festivals of thanksgiving we recognise the great work they have done and the abundance that they have brought us. We thank them and we join with them in their dances and communion. In sacred dance and circle dancing, we evoke and join the angelic celebration — and again we honour the Earth.

The Celtic Fire Festivals — Imbolc, Beltane, Lammas and Samhain

Intimately connected with the nature cycle that includes the Spring and Autumn Equinoxes are the Celtic festivals of Imbolc, Beltane, Lammas and Samhain. They are all concerned with the awakening of the forces of nature and with growth.

They are festivals which are frequently associated with fire for two reasons: 1. As symbolic of the energy of the Sun without which there would be no growth, for it is cosmic fire which is the source of all life. 2. Because fire is the three-dimensional 'real' life perceptual experience closest to the reality of the existence of nature spirits and angels. In the quiet of a church, the flame of a candle suffices to attract their helpful blessings and presence. In great fields, woods and pastures, fires are appropriate to call and celebrate the cooperation of the spirits of growth.

These Fire Festivals do not have precisely fixed dates as they vary according to geography and local ecology.

Imbolc, dated at around February 1st, is the first day of the Celtic Spring and celebrates the first sign that the nature devas are awakening. Imbolc is, in many ways, a call from humanity to the nature spirits. It is a call that is done with mysterious and considerate respect.

Beltane celebrates that the work of growth is fully on its way. It is usually dated around May 1st. The angels of the harvest are now confident that the process is in full swing and we can now celebrate that the proper momentum has been successfully achieved.

Lammas marks the first real sign of the fruit of their labours and the first day of the harvest. The whole cycle is proving to have been successful and once again a celebration is in order. This is usually dated around the 1st August.

Samhain occurs around the end of October and beginning of November. It is also known as the Peace-Fire and the end of the Celtic year. The great nature spirits are now fully in their cycle of inner contemplation. Their activity is now turned to peace. In recognition of this and the long nights ahead, we too enter into peace and contemplation. It is now many weeks until the Winter solstice and months until Spring with its great rebirth of natural growth and the great inner Festival of Wesak.

The Major Religions

It is also inspiring to attune in meditation to the rhythms of the world's major religions, becoming aware of their major Festivals. As a first step, one can attune to the inner rhythm of the major religion of one's own culture and then begin to investigate others. Some readers may think that I have not paid sufficient respect to the major religions, but they already have many thousands of books devoted to them. If you are comfortably located within a particular church, temple or belief, I have no desire to pull you away from it. All the meditation approaches in this book can be used to enrich your experience of the faith you already enjoy.

Meditation Schools

There are many meditation schools and if you would like to work with one, it is best to research your local area and to follow your own instinct and intuition. Many people have had a good start with Transcendental Meditation. You may have a local Buddhist group. Many churches today also have meditation groups. There are also two meditation schools I trust which work by post:

The Arcane School
3 Whitehall Court
Suite 54
London SW1A 2EF
 and
866 United Nations Plaza
Suite 566-7
New York - NY 10017-1888.

Meditation Group for the New Age
Sundial House
Nevill Court
Tunbridge Wells
Kent TN4 8NJ
 and
PO Box 566
Ojai
California 93023

Booklist

There are many many relevant books. Nearly every spiritual teacher has written something that is inspiring or enlightening about the subject. And there are hundreds of other books on meditation. Each of them will have something that is stimulating and helpful. It is best to follow one's own intuition in choosing what one reads. Here, however, is a list of a few that I think particularly helpful.

If you are having trouble with focus and concentration: Christmas Humphreys, *Concentration and Meditation*, many editions; Mouni Sadhu, *Concentration*, Mandala/Allen & Unwin.

For working with children: Deborah Rozman, *Meditating with Children*, University of the Trees.

For stimulation in expanding awareness and consciousness: Dion Fortune, *The Cosmic Doctrine*, Helios; Alice Bailey, *Esoteric Astrology*, Lucis Press; Jane Roberts, all the *Seth* books, Prentice Hall; Ken Wilber, *Spectrum of Consciousness*, Quest Books.

Psychological books that will help with self-reflection: John Rowan, *The Transpersonal in Counselling and Therapy*, Routledge; Dave Mearns & Windy Dryden, *Experiences of Counselling in Action*, Sage; Carl Rogers, *The Carl Rogers Reader*, Constable.

Some other books on meditation: Mouni Sadhu, *Meditation*, Allen & Unwin; Mouni Sadhu, *Samadhi*, Mandala/Allen & Unwin; Alice Bailey, *Letters on Occult Meditation*, Lucis Press; *Meditation for the New Age*, a course of six booklets, Sundial House/Meditation Group for the

New Age; Michael Eastcott, *The Silent Path*, Rider; Osel Tendzin, *Buddha in the Palm of Your Hand*, Shambhala; Yogi Ramacharaka, *A Series of Lessons in Raja Yoga*, Fowler; Lawrence LeShan, *How to Meditate*, Crucible.

For affirmations and seed thoughts: the books of Louise Hay; Parahamahansa Yogananda, *Metaphysical Meditations*, Self-Realization Fellowship; Parahamansa Yogananda, *Scientific Healing Affirmations*, Self-Realization Fellowship.

For general inspiration: The *Agni Yoga* series; *The Yoga Sutras of Patanjali*, many translations and editions but particularly the Alice Bailey translation, *The Light of the Soul*, Lucis Press; *The Bhagavad Gita*, many translations and editions; *A Course in Miracles*; William James, *The Varieties of Religious Experience*, Triumph.

Afterword

Whatever you may think of this book, the reason you have it in your hands is that you are interested in meditation. You may close and ignore this book, but something within you is calling you to sit in silence.

This call to silence is an invitation from your own soul, your true self, to come into closer relationship. It asks very little in return — only for moments of silence. If we have received this invitation to enter silence, is it not worth responding?

This being, who is the true self, waits patiently for intimacy.

There are cassettes available which accompany this book. For details of these and workshops, courses, other books and cassettes by William Bloom, please contact:

Alternatives
St. James's Church
197 Piccadilly
London W1V 9RF

Gothic Image Publications is a Glastonbury-based imprint dedicated to publishing books and pamphlets that offer a new and radical approach to our perception of ourselves and the world.

Current publications include:

The Avalonians
Patrick Benham

Conflict in the Caucasus
Svetlana Chervonnaya

Devas, Fairies and Angels
William Bloom

Dowsing the Crop Circles
edited by John Michell

Dragons: Their History and Symbolism
Janet Hoult

Glastonbury Abbey
James Carley

Glastonbury: Maker of Myths
Frances Howard-Gordon

The Glastonbury Tor Maze
Geoffrey Ashe

The Green Lady and the King of Shadows
Moyra Caldecott

Labyrinths: Ancient Myths and Modern Uses
Sig Lonegren

The Living World of Faery
R J Stewart

Needles of Stone Revisited
Tom Graves

The New Ley Hunter's Guide
Paul Devereux

New Light on the Ancient Mystery of Glastonbury
John Michell

Positively Wyrd: Harnessing the Chaos in your Life
Tom Graves

Robin Hood: Green Lord of the Wildwood
John Matthews

Sacred England
John Michell

The Sacred Magician: A Ceremonial Diary
William Bloom

Saint or Satan? The Life and Times of Russia's New Rasputin, Anatoly Kashpirovsky
Galina Vinogradova

Spiritual Dowsing
Sig Lonegren

Symbolic Landscapes: The Dreamtime Earth and Avebury's Open Secret
Paul Devereux

Gothic Image Publications are available from all good bookshops or direct from:

Gothic Image Publications
7 High Street
Glastonbury, Somerset   Telephone: +44 1458 831453
BA6 9DP   Fax: +44 1458 831666